CASE STUDIES

FOR

CARPET INSPECTORS

ISBN 0 9528610 0 3

April 1997

Printed in Great Britain by

FM Repro Ltd
Repro House, 69 Lumb Lane, Liversedge, West Yorkshire, W15 7NB, United Kingdom

Published by

CLEANING RESEARCH INTERNATIONAL LTD
49 Boroughgate, Otley, West Yorkshire, LS21 1AG, United Kingdom
Tel: 44 (0)1943 462389   Fax: 44 (0)1943 464316

PREFACE

The primary objective of this manual is to provide the carpet inspector with a number of illustrated examples and specimen reports based upon several actual case histories. A secondary objective is to provide a fundamental if somewhat superficial background to textile technology. Such aspects have been discussed only briefly, or not at all, in *The Identification of Carpet Faults* and *Diagnostic Techniques for the Investigation of Carpet Complaints*.

The manual is divided into four sections.

Section One is concerned with elementary textile technology. Every carpet inspector should have some understanding of the classification of textile fibres, their important characteristics, and how ultimately they are formed into yarn. They should also have a knowledge of certain terms that will enable them to add authority to their reports. Similarly, Section Two is concerned with carpet manufacture. Section Three details general principles to be followed when preparing a technical report, and Section Four, by means of examples, provides the background to a number of interesting cases supported, where appropriate, by technical discussion and several specimen reports.

Some cases are illustrated with photographs although for reasons of printing economy (and hence cost to the reader) the photographs do not appear alongside the report to which they relate but have been collected together at the end of the section.

The names have been changed to protect the innocent.

The author acknowledges *Wools of New Zealand* for permission to reprint certain diagrams, some of which may have originated in earlier publications from elsewhere.

CONTENTS

Page No.

LIST OF PLATES

SECTION ONE

AN INTRODUCTION TO TEXTILE TECHNOLOGY

FIBRE CLASSIFICATION

Textile Fibres are broadly classified into two categories - *natural* fibres and *man-made* fibres. Not all are used in carpets.

Natural fibres may be *animal, vegetable* or *mineral* in origin. The important members of the group are shown in Figure 1.

Figure 1.   Classification of natural fibres

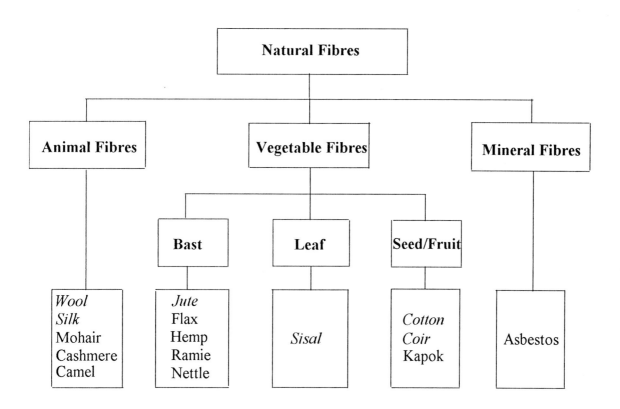

Animal fibres other than wool and silk are also known as *Specialty Hairs.*

Those fibres which may be used in floor coverings, either as pile or in the backing, are shown in italics. Wool is predominantly used as a pile fibre (although it may form the backing of some orientals); silk is only used in orientals. Jute and cotton are widely used as backing materials although even these may have some limited use as pile yarns. Coir is the fibre component of coconut matting whilst sisal enjoys occasional popularity as a fashion product.

Man-made fibres fall into two subdivisions. Those which are formed either from naturally occurring raw materials such as wood pulp, peanuts or soya and are known as *regenerated fibres*; and those which are created by chemical synthesis to produce *synthetic* fibres. These are summarised by Figure 2.

Figure 2. *Classification of man-made fibres*

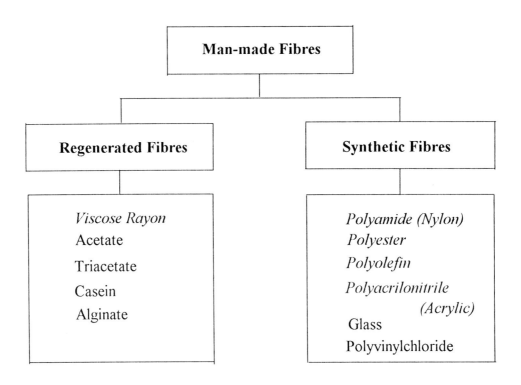

The classification given in this figure is capable of additional refinement but such detail goes beyond the scope of this book.

Historically regenerated fibres came first with the development in the middle of the nineteenth century of an explosive substance with fibrous properties known as nitrocellulose. The process was further refined by Sir Joseph Swan to provide filaments for the newly invented light bulb. Then, at the turn of the century British patents were taken out on a fibre closely resembling viscose rayon as we know it today. For a number of years, especially in the sixties and seventies when wall to wall carpeting was becoming accessible to the masses, the fibre was used alone or more commonly in blends to produce cheaper qualities of carpet that were affordable by all. Because the fibre has low abrasion resistance however, such carpets had extremely poor wear characteristics and with the development of other tougher synthetics for use in carpet yarns the fibre is now seldom seen, except perhaps in some low quality orientals pretending to be something they are not. Polyolefin is the cheap fibre of the nineties.

Let us now consider in greater detail those fibres from both categories which may be used in carpet manufacture.

Fibre Production

Whilst there is a certain similarity about the manufacture of all the man-made fibres, there is considerable variety in the origins of the natural fibres. This variety may well be the reason why the properties and characteristics of the natural fibres are in many ways, somewhat unique.

Wool

Wool grows in a range of fibre diameters and a range of fibre lengths. It also differs in degrees of crimpiness and in colour. The characteristics of a fleece are defined by the technical term *Quality*. In general terms, those qualities which comprise fine long fibres are used for apparel fabrics such as worsted suiting and lightweight hosiery. Such fleeces come mainly from *Merino* sheep by far the greatest producer of which is Australia followed by South Africa. There are no Merino breeds indigenous to the UK because they are unable to tolerate the climate. (A fact demonstrated in 1787 when several rams and 36 ewes sent by the King of Spain as a present to George III, failed to survive).

Coarser qualities, often (but not always) shorter in fibre length, are obtained from the so-called *Crossbred* breeds which represent by far the greatest proportion of sheep in the world today. Within this grouping, the coarsest strongest wools are produced from *Carpet* breeds, typically mountain sheep with wool coarser than 35 microns in diameter.

Perhaps the most important producer of carpet wools is New Zealand who arguably produce the best wools within this classification. New Zealand wools are strong, clean and uniform in staple. Carpet wools are also produced in the UK, South America and the Commonwealth of Russian States amongst others, although in the case of the latter few Russian wools are used by carpet manufacturers in the EU, US or Australasia.

After shearing, wool is baled and then shipped for subsequent cleaning (*scouring*), disentangling (*carding*) and spinning into yarn.

Silk

Silk is produced by the caterpillar of the *bombyx mori* species of moth, the commonly used term 'silkworm' being something of a misnomer. The fibre is extruded through two holes on either side of the caterpillar's head as it spins itself a cocoon for metamorphosis into an adult moth. One caterpillar produces two filaments each up to 1.5 km long, bound together by a sticky glue like substance known as *seracin*.

Before metamorphosis is complete the chrysalis is killed by baking in the sun or a hot oven, or by stifling in hot air or steam.

To obtain the fibre, the cocoons are soaked in hot water to soften the gum, then using a revolving brush to find the end of the filament, several are combined together and reeled in a skilful operation to produce a multi-filament yarn. Subsequent degumming removes the remaining seracin gum the bulk of which at this stage, still remains.

JUTE

Jute is a *bast* fibre of the *corchorus* genus. Bast fibres are obtained from the stems of woody plants usually as a fibrous layer just beneath the bark. The purpose of such fibres is to hold the plant erect. Grown to heights of 5m or so in India and Bangladesh the plants are harvested annually usually by hand sickle.

The strands of fibres are separated from the woody and cellular components of the plant by a controlled process of rotting, known as *retting*. This usually involves steeping the stalks in a slow moving stream or dam and allowing the fibrous components to separate out by a process of biological degradation. Daily examination ensures that the degradation does not go too far. When the strands of fibre can easily be separated from the stem, they are washed and then hung in the sun to dry before shipping for spinning.

SISAL

Sisal is a *leaf* fibre from the *agave sisalana* plant originating originally in Central America, although now grown in East Africa, Mexico, Haiti and parts of South America. As the name suggests the fibres are obtained from the leaf of the plant. Leaves are harvested when the plant is typically three years old and continues until it flowers and dies (after about seven years). A plant may yield 400,000 fibres during its lifetime.

The fibres are separated from the pulpy material that surrounds them by machine scraping and are then washed and dried and bleached in the sun or in ovens before shipping and dyeing for use in twines and sacks and - as fashion dictates - in floor coverings.

COTTON

In the carpet industry cotton tends to be used only in backing materials. It is also used extensively for upholstery fabrics and is an extremely important fibre for apparel.

Cotton is a seed fibre, growing in the seed pods or *bolls* of plants of the *possypium* genus. As the plant matures the bolls burst to reveal the cotton fibres, as many as 150,000 fibres in each boll (20,000 per seed). The bolls may be picked mechanically or by hand and the fibres are then separated mechanically from the seeds by a process known as ginning. The fibres are then cleaned, typically by opening and beating, and finally carded and spun.

VISCOSE

Viscose Rayon is a regenerated cellulose fibre commonly made from wood pulp or *cotton linters* - fragments of cotton fibres often with seeds attached, too short for use in the production of cotton yarn.

The wood pulp comes from selected tree species which are rich in cellulose including northern spruce, eucalyptus and certain pines. During manufacture the wood pulp is converted into alkali cellulose (using caustic soda) which is then shredded and allowed to age. After ageing the crumbs are digested with carbon disulphide to form sodium cellulose xanthate which is then added to caustic soda and allowed to ripen at a controlled temperature. When the carefully controlled ripening process is complete the mixture is pumped through the tiny jets of a spinneret into a bath of sulphuric acid, sodium sulphate and zinc sulphate to produce viscose fibre ready for subsequent spinning. Used extensively in apparel and some upholstery fabrics it is now virtually unknown in carpets.

NYLON

Today, nylon is the most common of all carpet pile fibres.

Nylon is a polyamide. That is to say it is a polymer in which a recurrent component of the chemical structure is an amide group. (Wool and silk are naturally occurring polyamides).

Typically, nylon is produced by one of two different routes although the resultant chemical structures are quite similar. One route involves reacting a diamine, such as hexamethylene diamine, with a dibasic acid like adipic acid to produce polyhexamethylene adipamide or nylon 6.6. The other route involves self-condensation of an amino acid or derivative like caprolactam to produce nylon 6. There are slight differences in end use performance of the two products.

To form the fibre, the raw materials are heated until they melt and are then forced through the holes of a spinneret where they coagulate in a stream of cold air. Steam is then introduced to increase the moisture content, making the fibre more stable and a slight amount of twist is inserted. Finally the filaments are stretched (or *drawn*) to reorientate the molecules down the length of the filament thereby imparting characteristic lustre and strength to the fibre.

The fibre may be spun into continuous filament yarn or may be chopped into shorter lengths and spun as staple yarn. In staple form it is commonly blended with wool to complement the resilience of wool with the strength and durability of the nylon.

POLYOLEFIN

A fibre of increasing importance for use both as a pile yarn and a backing yarn. Polypropylene is the most common polyolefin although polyethylene, often known as polythene, enjoys a wide variety of non-fibrous uses. It is made by polymerisation of olefin hydrocarbons, typically ethylene and propylene, - raw materials obtained from the oil industry.

Techniques of fibre production do not differ significantly from the melt spinning technique used for nylon and the fibre is available in both continuous filament and staple format.

ACRYLIC

Acrylic fibres, or more accurately, polyacrilonitrile fibres are in fact usually a mixture of two polymers of which at least 85% is acrylonitrile monomer. Melt spinning of the type used for the production of nylon and polypropylene is not suitable for acrylic fibres because the polymer is unstable when heated. The fibre therefore has to be produced by dry spinning or wet spinning. Both involve dissolution of the polymer in dimethylformamide (or some other suitable solvent). In dry spinning techniques the resultant solution is boiled before extruding through spinnerets into hot air or gas (up to 400°C) which evaporates the solvent to produce filaments of acrylonitrile fibre. In wet spinning the polymer is dissolved in solvent and then pumped into a coagulating bath of a compound in which the solvent is soluble but in which the acrylonitrile fibre is not. As is the case with nylon and polypropylene, the fibres are drawn to reorientate the molecules and may then be processed as continuous filament or as staple fibre.

POLYESTER

The use of polyester as a carpet fibre tends to be more subject to fashion trends than any of the other carpet fibres. It is made by condensing ethylene glycol with terephthallic acid or dimethyl terephthalate to produce polyethylene terephthalate which is more commonly known as polyester. As is the case with nylon and polypropylene, the fibre is melt spun by heating the polymer up to around 260°C before extrusion through the spinneret. In the case of polyester however great care is taken to exclude oxygen from the melt since this would destabilise the polymer.

Again the filaments are drawn after extrusion to orientate the molecules and impart strength. They may then be processed into continuous filament or staple fibre yarns.

FIBRE CHARACTERISTICS

Every carpet inspector should have some understanding of the principal fibre characteristics. He needs to know for example that wool fibres are unaffected by sulphuric acid whereas nylon fibres dissolve. That car battery acid for example will have no effect on a polypropylene backed 100% wool carpet but will dissolve the nylon pile and jute and cotton backing yarns in an 80% wool / 20 % nylon jute backed carpet.

Table 1 summarises some of the major fibre characteristics.

Table 1.   Summary of Fibre Characteristics

Effect of:	Wool	Nylon	Polypropylene	Acrylic	Polyester	Cotton	Jute
Heat	Decomposes at 130°C. Chars at 300°C with smell of burning feathers.	Melts around 250°C (nylon 6.6) or 215°C (nylon 6).	Softens around 150°C and melts at approx 170°C. Shrinks from flame.	Discolours with heat. burns with acrid fumes.	Good resistance, softens around 260°C.	Decomposes at 150°C. Burns readily with smell of burning paper.	Burns readily
Sunlight	Slowly degrades, becomes yellow and loses strength.	Very slow loss of strength.	Degrades in presence of oxygen in air but can easily be stabilised.	Excellent resistance.	Good resistance.	Slow loss of strength and fibre yellows.	Not seriously affected unless in the presence of moisture.
Acids	Not generally affected but will dissolve in hot concentrated sulphuric.	Completely degrades in cold concentrated mineral acids and affected by dilute mineral acids. Dissolves in 80% formic acid.	Unaffected.	Not affected by dilute mineral acids but may dissolve if exposed to concentrated acids for long periods	Good resistance to mineral acids.	Dissolves in hot concentrated and cold dilute mineral acids.	Attacked by mineral acids.

Table 1. Summary of Fibre Characteristics (Continued)

Effect of:	Wool	Nylon	Polypropylene	Acrylic	Polyester	Cotton	Jute
Alkalis	Affected by most alkalis and dissolves in caustic soda.	Unaffected.	Unaffected.	Attacked by strong alkalis.	Generally resistance though may hydrolyse at extreme temperature under pressure.	Excellent resistance to alkalis.	Degraded by alkalis which in carpets can promote cellulosic browning.
Organic Solvents	Not generally affected.	Dissolves in phenol and cresol.	Unaffected.	Generally resistant to common solvents. Dissolve in hot dimethylform-amide.	Excellent resistance to most common solvents.	Unaffected by common organic solvents.	Unaffected
Insects	Damaged by certain species.	Unaffected.	Unaffected.	Unaffected.	Unaffected.	Unaffected.	Unaffected
Mildew and Bacteria	Degraded.	Unaffected.	Unaffected.	Unaffected.	Unaffected.	Degraded.	Degraded but less readily than cotton

FROM FIBRE TO YARN

Conversion of fibre to yarn follows one of a small number of routes that though similar are not exactly the same. The differences depend upon the fibre type being processed. It is not within the scope of this manual to consider every aspect of yarn preparation however and we shall therefore be concerned only with the preparation of pile yarns from major pile fibre types.

Three distinct phases may be involved in the conversion of fibre to yarn:

- ❑ cleaning
- ❑ disentanglment
- ❑ spinning

Let us consider each in turn.

CLEANING

Of the major pile fibres wool is the one that requires some form of preliminary cleaning. Raw wool is contaminated with grease, dirt, urine, and sweat. In some cases vegetable material in the form of *burrs* - seed cases and pieces of grass and thorn, may also have become caught up in the fleece whilst still on the hoof.

The process of cleaning is known as *scouring* and involves passing the dirty fleeces through baths of detergent or soap and alkali to remove almost all of the contaminants. If the raw material is badly affected by vegetable contaminants it may also be necessary to *carbonise* the scoured wool. This involves steeping in dilute sulphuric acid, baking and crushing.

It is important that scouring is carried out effectively. If too high a level of residual wool grease remains on the fibre after conversion to yarn the carpet is likely to exhibit the phenomenon of rapid soiling. Thus, a complaint that the carpet has become dirty in all trafficked areas should flag up to the inspector the possibility that scouring has been inadequate. A suitably equipped laboratory can not only confirm that the level of oily material is outside commercially acceptable tolerances, but can establish whether the 'oil' is wool grease or residual processing lubricant applied at some later stage of processing.

DISENTANGLEMENT

Fibres which are processed in staple form i.e. wool and synthetics which have been chopped into short lengths, need to pass through some form of disentaglement process. This technique is known as *carding* and is the first in a series of operations intended to parallelise the fibres in a suitable way to present them for subsequent spinning.

In simple terms a carding machine - often referred to as a *card,* is a large cylinder of some 2 metres in diameter, closely covered in hard, sharp pointed wires. A series of rollers, similarly clothed in wire, is arranged around the external surface of the main cylinder such that as the cylinder and rollers rotate, the wires intermesh to provide a tearing action. This tearing action disentangles the fibres which are fed into the machine by means of a *hopper.* As the carding process reaches equilibrium, fibres pass back and forth between the swift and the various rollers until eventually, and quite randomly, they are stripped off by the doffer roller and are delivered as a thin, fibrous web some 2 metres wide. A schematic representation of a woollen card is shown in Figure 3.

Figure 3.   Schematic representation of a woollen card

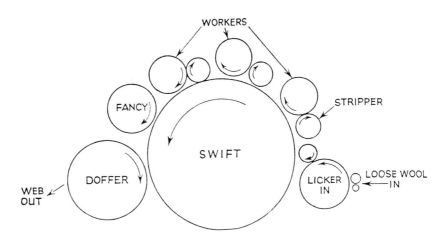

In woollen carding (which defines the equipment rather than the fibre being processed) the fibrous web is split into continuous strips along its length which are slightly rolled together to give some cohesion before spooling onto a bobbin. This so-called *roving* is then ready for one of various spinning processes.

Carding is usually preceded by *blending*. This is the process by which different components of the yarn are mixed together in the correct proportions required in the finished yarn. Blending may simply involve the mixing of various types of wool (from different breeds thereby imparting a variety of characteristics of crimp bulk and colour into the finished yarn); the mixing of different types of staple fibre such as wool and nylon; or the mixing of *stock dyed* material (q.v.) to produce a certain colourway such as a heather mix for example. The intimacy of the final blend is improved by the carding operation.

Carding is of course omitted from the processing of continuous filament synthetic fibres.

SPINNING.

The principles involved in spinning are fundamentally simple. There are two aspects, *attenuation* or drawing out, and *twisting*. In layman's terms the attenuation causes the yarn to become leaner and the twisting holds it together. In due course several yarns may be twisted or *plied* together by a process known as *folding* to create typically a two- ply *(two-fold)* or three-ply *(three-fold)* yarn. *Setting*, using heat, steam or chemicals depending upon the fibre type then gives stability to the yarn, an important aspect if the yarn is to be used in cut pile carpets since setting stops the pile from fuzzing and bursting. In the so-called *hard twist* yarns, higher levels of twist and degrees of setting are imparted to help the yarn retain its characteristic tight and springy appearance in the finished product.

At these various stages of processing, blending, carding, spinning and folding, it is not unusual to provide some form of lubrication, usually in the form of water soluble oils. Additionally, man-made fibres are often lubricated with *spin finish* as they are wound from the spinneret from which they are extruded during manufacture. These oils are removed in some subsequent stage of processing, eg dyeing. Failure to remove them to an adequately low level may result in rapid soiling in traffic lanes. Failure to remove them consistently across all yarns in the blend will result in soiling as stripes in the finished carpet.

DYEING

The coloration of carpet yarns may take place at a number of different points in the processing cycle. These include:

- ❑ Before the extrusion of man made fibres - known as *solution dyeing*
- ❑ Before carding - *stock dyeing*
- ❑ After spinning - *yarn dyeing* for which there are a number of techniques

Additionally, the carpet itself may be coloured by:

- ❑ Dyeing after manufacture or *piece dyeing*
- ❑ *Screen printing* or less commonly, *roller printing* techniques
- ❑ The injection of colour by jets of dye directed through needles to each individual tuft by an unusual technique specific to one carpet manufacturer

Dyes are themselves divided into a number of *classes*. For example them may be described as *acid dyes, basic dyes, premetallised dyes, vat dyes, disperse dyes* and so on. Different classes will react with (said to be *substantive to*) different fibres. For example nylon is usually dyed with acid dyes (although basic dyeable nylon is also manufactured). Wool may be dyed with acid dyes, basic dyes, premetallised dyes; acrylics with basic dyes and so forth. The *substantivity* of different dyes is dependent upon the reactive groups in the fibre's molecular structure and upon the conditions under which the dye is applied.

SOLUTION DYEING

In the case of solution dyeing, the raw material used to manufacture man made fibres is mixed with coloured pigments before extrusion takes place. Thus, when the fibre is produced it is already coloured. Colours produced in this way are extremely stable and are not affected by bleaches. Because of its inertness and its hydrophilic character, polyolefin fibres are almost always coloured in this way. Solution dyed nylon is also manufactured offering long term stain release warranties. The disadvantage of solution dyeing is that the range of available colours tends to be limited, and, in the case of nylon, the fibre tends to be more receptive to stains even if the stains are easier to remove. (This is because, never having been immersed in a dye vessel many dye reactive groups which are present on the surface of the fibre are unreacted. If then an acid dye, like coffee, is spilled onto the carpet the fibre has a greater affinity than is the case with a conventionally dyed nylon). With a conventionally dyed nylon however, removal techniques are highly likely to remove the dye that is intended to be there, resulting in an overall loss of colour from the fibre. If it is solution dyed, the stain can usually be successfully discharged without any deleterious effect on the colour.

STOCK DYEING

Stock dyeing involves dyeing the fibre whilst in raw material form, usually before blending and always before carding. Fibres may be dyed to what is notionally the same colour to produce a yarn of one single shade, or they may be dyed in different colours to produce a yarn such as a heather mix for example. If the resultant yarn is a mix of fibre types it is unlikely that the different fibres will dye to exactly the same shade however. Even when the raw material is the same fibre type different dye uptake between blend components should be expected (because the components are likely to differ slightly in physicochemical constitution). This possibility further highlights the importance of ensuring that the blending operation is as efficient as possible.

YARN DYEING

Yarn dyeing may be carried out in hank (US skein), or on some form of *package* i.e. wound onto a bobbin or cone, often with perforated cores through which dye liquor may be pumped. Again it is important that the dyer considers the different dyeing characteristics of the different components of the blend so that he can produce yarn of the correct resultant colour. For example if a wool and nylon blend is being dyed to a brown shade the individual fibres in the blend will have different substantivities for the dyes being used. Thus it is quite likely that the wool and the nylon components of the yarn will not be of exactly the same colour when the dyeing process is complete. If the divergence in colour is too great then during wear, as the weaker fibre wears preferentially there is a strong likelihood that the carpet will change shade in the traffic lanes from that of the resultant colour of the yarn to that of the colour of the stronger fibre. The diligent inspector will be wary of this possibility.

Whichever of the above routes are followed, the yarn is presented to the carpet manufacturer in coloured form. However, in some cases the carpet is manufactured from undyed yarn. The resultant carpet is then dyed in its continuous length.

PIECE DYEING

Piece dyeing involves dyeing the finished carpet *in the piece* as an endless loop i.e. when it has been fully constructed as a carpet.

One problem facing the carpet dyer is the large volumes of liquor that are required. This may be overcome by treating the carpet in open width using foam applications of dyes. However such systems give poor penetration. Spray techniques avoid the excessive amounts of liquor that are required for conventional piece dyeing and also give better penetration than foam techniques.

Although the manufacturer may have a few tricks available to him, it is customary when a carpet is piece dyed for it to finish up in a solid shade. (He may subsequently overprint a pattern or may *discharge print* a pattern, which involves taking the dyed carpet and creating a pattern by preferentially bleaching out areas of yarn to produce a patterned effect).

PRINTING

Printing carpets is similar to printing fabrics. They may be *screen* printed or *roller* printed.

Printing is critically dependent upon the depth of penetration of the print paste. If it is inadequate, dye will not penetrate sufficiently down the length of the tuft and white uncoloured fibres may 'grin through' to the surface. Even if penetration is adequate any fibre migration, because of low tuft bind for example, may result in an overall lightening and loss of definition of the pattern as uncoloured portions of fibres migrate to the surface.

Screen printing gives excellent possibilities for patterning since, theoretically at least, there is no restriction on the number of colours that may be used. It also provides an opportunity to apply intricate patterns to tufted carpets. However, the capital outlay and space requirements of a carpet printing plant are high as are the volumes and hence cost of the water that is used.

In roller printing the scope of the design is somewhat limited and the cost of engraving rollers is high. Nevertheless, the technique is used extensively in the patterning of flocked carpets where it is customary to stock dye the (nylon) fibre to a single or bicomponent shade and then to roller print over the top.

Further Reading

W J Onions   *Wool, an introduction to its properties, varieties, uses and production.*
                        Benn 1962

J Gordon Cook   *Handbook of Textile Fibres I - Natural Fibres*
                        Merrow 1993   ISBN 0 904095 39 8

J Gordon Cook   *Handbook of Textile Fibres II - Man-Made Fibres*
                        Merrow 1993   ISBN 0 904095 40 1

W Ingamells   *Colour for Textiles - a user's handbook*
                        Society of Dyers and Colourists 1993   ISBN 0 901956 56 2

Section Two

An Introduction to Carpet Manufacture

There are a surprisingly large number of different ways by which carpets may be manufactured. These include:

- ❑ Weaving
- ❑ Tufting
- ❑ Bonding
- ❑ Flocking
- ❑ Hand Knotting
- ❑ Knitting

Weaving and Tufting are the two most important and we shall consider these in the greatest detail. Of these two, weaving is the oldest technique and the most complex.

WEAVING

One simple way to categorise woven carpets as distinct from those produced by other techniques is to describe them as carpets where the entire structure of pile and backing is assembled simultaneously in a single operation. This offers considerable flexibility in terms of patterning but suffers the disadvantage that production rates are low. There are two fundamental techniques; *Axminster* weaving, and *Wilton* weaving, (which also includes *Face-to-Face* weaving). Within each category are some minor subdivisions which relate to certain characteristics of the production process. Let us consider each in a little more detail.

AXMINSTERS

Axminster carpets offer a number of benefits. Most notable is their potential for variety of colour and design. Additionally they are cost effective in their use of pile yarn (unlike Wilton carpets where a large proportion of the pile yarn may be hidden beneath the surface of the pile); patterns of textures, as well as colours are possible; designs may be easily customised to a clients particular requirements, and they are especially suitable for use with wool.

Typical Axminster weave structures are shown in Figure 4 in which the term *shot* refers to the number of weft insertions of the backing per row of tufts across the carpet. It will be seen that in those weaves described as *Kardax* weaves, the design may be seen on the back. This is not the case with *Corinthian* weaves.

There are three different techniques by which Axminsters may be woven, and these depend upon the operating principles of the loom. They are known as:

- ❑ Gripper-Jacquard Weaving
- ❑ Spool-Gripper Weaving
- ❑ Spool Weaving

Spool Axminster weaving is still used today but such looms are no longer manufactured and the technique is therefore becoming less common.

Figure 4.   Typical Axminster weave structures.

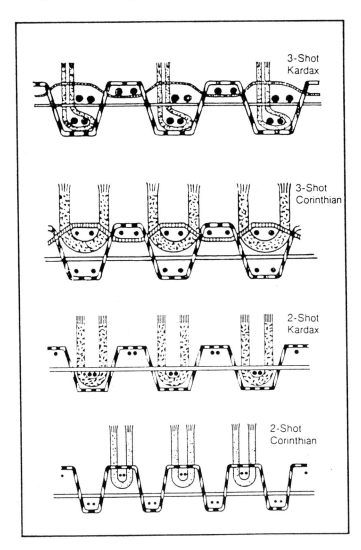

GRIPPER-JACQUARD AXMINSTER WEAVING

In order to understand the principles of Gripper-Jacquard Axminster weaving, it is first necessary to explain a number of technical terms. The descriptions which follow are not to be considered as definitions however and as such may not satisfy the textile technologist. Rather, they are intended for the layman in an attempt to make a difficult concept more lucid. The necessary terms are as follows:

Yarn Package: Yarn wound onto cone shaped bobbins. The conical shape facilitates unwinding as weaving proceeds.

Packages may have different configurations for different textile purposes. For example they may have perforated centres for dyeing. They may have parallel sides with circular flanges at the top and bottom - the traditional bobbin shape - for some intermediate spinning operations. For carpet weaving purposes they are conical.

Creel: A creel is the racking system which stands behind the loom (or tufting machine in the case of tufted carpet production). Typically it is a steel structure and bears several thousand fixed spindles upon which the packages are placed for presentation of the yarn to the loom. In Gripper-Jacquard Axminster weaving it normally comprises several *frames* or rows of racking - one for each colour if multicoloured carpets are being produced. In the case of an eight colour design there will be eight frames of different colours. In a twelve colour design, there will be twelve.

Jacquard: A jacquard is a mechanism for patterning. Today electronic jacquards are available but the original system, still in use in many mills, is based upon a series of punched cards. These control the sequence of yarn selection on the loom and provide the intelligence by which the pattern is introduced. In the case of the more traditional mechanical punched card systems the presence, or lack of a hole in the card determines the correct yarn selection at the weaving point.

Yarn carrier: There is one yarn carrier for each tuft insertion point across the entire width of the loom. Typically it comprises a vertical holder threaded with one yarn from each of the frames on the creel. Thus, in an eight frame creel there will be eight yarn guides in the yarn carrier and in a twelve frame creel there will be twelve guides in the carrier. The yarn carrier is controlled by the jacquard.

Gripper: Figure 5 shows a schematic representation of a gripper. It is the device which grips the yarn selected by the jacquard for delivery to the weaving point. Note that the gripper is similar in cross section to a bird's head and indeed it is the 'beak' which takes the yarn from the yarn carrier. There is one gripper for each yarn carrier and hence one for each tuft insertion point across the entire width of the loom.

Figure 5.   Schematic representation of a gripper mechanism

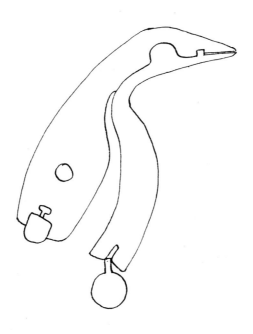

Let us then consider the sequence of events to produce one row of tufts across the width of the loom as illustrated by Figure 6.

Figure 6.   *Schematic representation of Gripper Jacquard yarn insertion mechanism.*

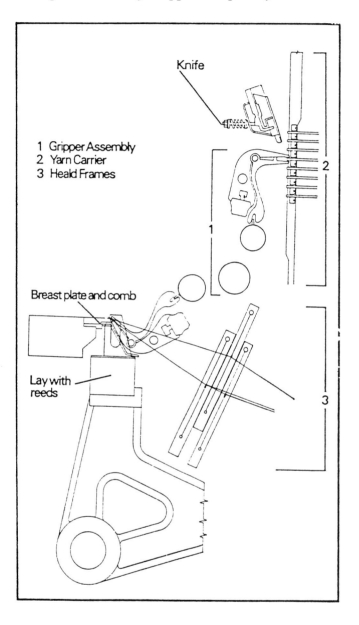

The process begins with the jacquard. The presence or absence of a hole in the punched card (or the action of a solenoid in the case of an electronic jacquard) determines, for every single tuft across the width of the machine, which colour should be presented by the yarn carrier to the gripper mechanism. Thus the jacquard determines the degree of vertical movement of every yarn carrier across the width. As one, all of the grippers reach forward, the jaws open and an end of yarn is gripped from the yarn carrier. The jaws close on the yarn and the grippers begin to rock backwards, withdrawing the yarns as they move. Once a predetermined length of yarn has been withdrawn (dependent upon the proposed tuft length) a blade operates across the whole width of the loom, cutting the yarns into individual tufts. The gripper mechanism then continues to rock backwards to the weft insertion point at which time the shuttle is whipped across the loom, binding one end of the tuft in place as the weft interlaces with the *chains* and *stuffers* of the warp[1]. The grippers then begin to return forward placing the other leg of the tufts in position to be bound in by another *shot* of the weft, the jaws finally opening to release the tuft and in anticipation of gripping the next end of yarn as presented by the yarn carrier.

SPOOL-GRIPPER AXMINSTER WEAVING

In Spool-Gripper Weaving the yarns for presentation to the grippers are held on spools which are similar to large bobbins, 36 inches in length (or one metre on a loom of metric dimensions). These are held by a *fret* or frame, which extends across the width of the loom. On a twelve foot loom therefore, four spools are arranged side by side in the fret. The frets are suspended by a chain from a gantry or harness, over the top of the loom. For a pattern that repeats over say 100 rows in the carpet there will be 100 frets, (or some multiple of 100) on the gantry. A multiple of four sets is normally considered to be an acceptable minimum.

Each spool is wound with yarns in the colour sequence demanded by the pattern. Thus, if the first tuft in the design is pink then the first yarn on the first spool will be pink. If the second tuft in the design is green, then the adjacent yarn on the first spool will be green; and so on across the width of the loom.

Each end of yarn on the spool is then threaded through its own individual tube on a tube frame. There is one tube frame per spool.

In spool-gripper weaving, there are spools in place of a creel and yarn carriers present the yarn to the grippers. The chain brings the frets of spools to the weaving position ready for selection by the grippers. The weaving mechanism is then similar to that of a gripper-jacquard, the yarns each being selected by a separate gripper which rocks back and implants the tuft at the weaving point.

After the first row of tufts has been inserted and the grippers begin to move up to select the next series of tufts for the next row in the design, the chain brings a new fret of spools to the yarn selection position. And so the cycle continues.

Clearly, it is most important that the spools are wound in the correct sequence to coincide with every row of the pattern and spool winding is a laborious and exacting skill. Weaving from spools does offer greater opportunity to have a large number of colours in the design however.

---

[1] In textile production the yarn that is inserted by the shuttle (or equivalent) is known as the *weft* and this traverses *across* the direction of production. The yarns which are arranged *in* the direction of production are known as the warp. In woven carpet manufacture *shots* of weft backing yarn interlace with *chains* of warp. *Stuffer* yarns which are inserted in the warp direction serve as spacers and provide dimensional stability to the structure. The chains may be manufactured from cotton, polypropylene or polyester, the stuffers from cotton, jute or polypropylene, and the weft from jute or polypropylene.

Spool-Gripper weaving is faster than Gripper-Jacquard weaving because in the former, both the distance travelled by the gripper is shorter and the delay necessary to manoeuvre the jacquard mechanism is avoided.

SPOOL AXMINSTER WEAVING

Spool Axminster looms are no longer made although some are still in production. The principle of operation is similar to that of the Spool-Gripper machine except that instead of grippers being used to bring the yarns to the weaving point the whole spool with its tube frame is brought into position. Clearly, production rates by this technique are slow - slower than either of the other two methods but, theoretically, there is no limit on the number of colours that may be used in the design.

FINISHING

Whichever Axminster technique is used it is customary to back-coat the carpet with a film of latex to increase tuft bind, and dimensional stability and decrease the fraying of raw edges when the carpet is cut. The pile is also inspected and mended if necessary and is brushed and cropped.

WILTONS

Let us first consider the more traditional Wilton weaving technique using a wireloom. Carpets manufactured in this way are particularly suited to contract use because of the capabilities of achieving low dense piles with a high resultant product weight and a firm handle. Wilton weaving using a wireloom also gives the opportunity to produce carpets in either cut or loop or cut and loop constructions with a variety of textures and up to five colours *(five frame)* although for reasons of cost two or three colours is more customary.

As is the case with gripper-jacquard Axminsters the yarn is fed from packages on a creel (or frame). In a multicoloured *(multiframe)* Wilton, a jacquard mechanism selects the correct yarns across the entire width of the machine and by raising them, lays them across a *wire* which meanwhile has been mechanically inserted also across the entire width of the machine. The jacquard selects the pile yarns in such a way as to make up one complete widthways row of the pattern. Yarns on the creel that are not required for that row of the pattern are not raised and ultimately become 'buried' beneath the surface pile in the backing of the carpet. It is these buried yarns which give the carpet its weight and dimensional stability but which also increase the cost of the carpet. The shuttle containing the weft backing yarn then whips across, interlacing with the warp backing yarns and binds the pile into place. By now other wires have been laid across the width of the machine and a new yarn selection has taken place by the jacquard.

There may be some 20 to 50 wires in a set and in due course those inserted at the beginning of the cycle begin to withdraw, ready for reinsertion during the next sequence. If the carpet is a cut pile construction the end of the wires is fitted with a blade which cuts the loops as it is withdrawn. In a loop pile construction (as in a *Brussels Wilton*), the wires are oval in cross section without any blade at the end.

Figure 7 shows a typical two shot single frame Brussels construction whilst Figure 8 represents a four frame two shot cut pile Wilton.

Figure 7.   Typical 2 -shot Brussels Wilton construction

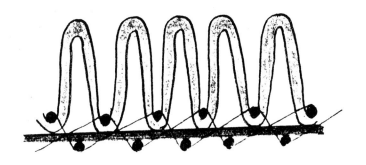

Figure 8.   Four frame 2 - shot cut pile Wilton construction.

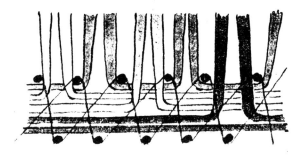

Wilton carpets are more stable than Axminsters but may still benefit from back-sizing.

FACE -TO-FACE WEAVING

Of the various weaving techniques, face-to-face weaving offers the greatest productivity. This is because, in effect, it provides a means of producing two carpets simultaneously. The technique is particularly useful for producing woven rugs from fine pile yarns to traditional handmade designs although coarser yarns may also be used to produce wall-to-wall carpeting. Loop pile constructions, and carpets of varying pile heights are not possible however (as they are with conventional wireloom Wiltons). The two carpets are of course mirror images of each other and are usually multicoloured with four or five colours in the design, selected using a jacquard mechanism. Up to seven colours are possible in the design.

Although some variations of technique are possible the same basic principle applies. It involves producing two carpets one above the other (and facing each other) with pile yarn shared between the two. The carpets are then separated by a sharp knife which reciprocates across the width of the machine. A schematic representation of a simple structure is shown in Figure 9.

Figure 9   *Schematic representation of a face-to-face woven construction.*

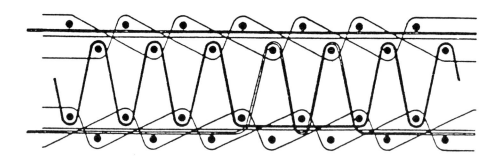

Back-sizing is desirable in the production of face-to-face carpets

TUFTING

Whereas in weaving the backing material and the pile is assembled simultaneously, in tufting a preformed backing is prepared before the pile is made. Tufting does not take place on a loom since a loom is a weaving machine. Tufting is carried out on a tufting machine.

Since its introduction tufting has gained rapid popularity because its high production rates have reduced the cost of manufacturing and have thus made wall-to-wall carpets accessible to all. In the early years, only plain or striped carpets were possible but with the introduction of sophisticated patterning mechanisms, tufted carpets are now able to offer an ever increasing variety of patterning options.

Tufting involves the needling of pile yarns through a backing material. A variety of preformed backings are available for this purpose . That through which the tufts are needled is known as the *primary backing*. This is typically a loosely woven fabric commonly made from polypropylene, or it may be a fibrous polypropylene scrim or web similar to the web which emerges from the doffer roller of a carding machine. Other similar types of structure may be used.

The backing stands on roll at the back of the machine and is fed over a roller to the tufting position. Here, across the entire width of the machine are the needles, each threaded with yarn delivered through tubes from packages on a creel, also at the rear of the machine. The needles, as one, penetrate the backing taking the yarn through with then. At this moment a *looper* is inserted between the eye of each needle and the yarn (the eye being near the point like the eye on a sewing machine needle). As the needles withdraw, a loop of pile is retained on the looper, the primary backing moves forward a small amount, and the needles penetrate the backing once more to insert a second row of tufts across the width of the machine.

This sequence produces a loop pile construction. A cut pile product is created by incorporating a knife within the looper.

Unlike woven carpets (excepting face-to-face constructions) which are made face up, in the case of tufting it is the back of the carpet that is seen when viewed from the stitching position, Figure 10 shows the tufting process schematically. Figures 11 and 12 illustrate the sequence of events in the production of loop pile and of cut pile tufted carpets.

Figure 10   Schematic representation of tufting process

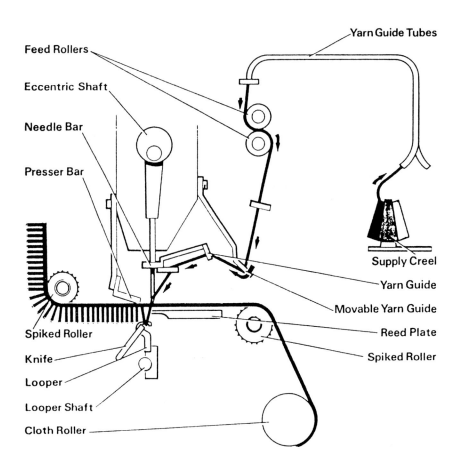

Figure 11.   *Sequence of operations in loop pile tufted production*

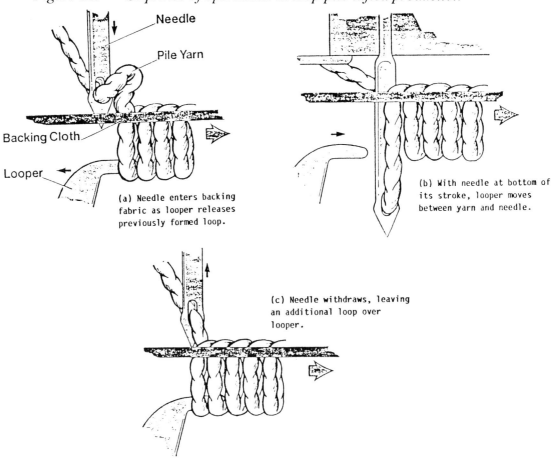

Needle

Pile Yarn

Backing Cloth

Looper

(a) Needle enters backing fabric as looper releases previously formed loop.

(b) With needle at bottom of its stroke, looper moves between yarn and needle.

(c) Needle withdraws, leaving an additional loop over looper.

Figure 12.   *Sequence of operations in cut pile tufted production*

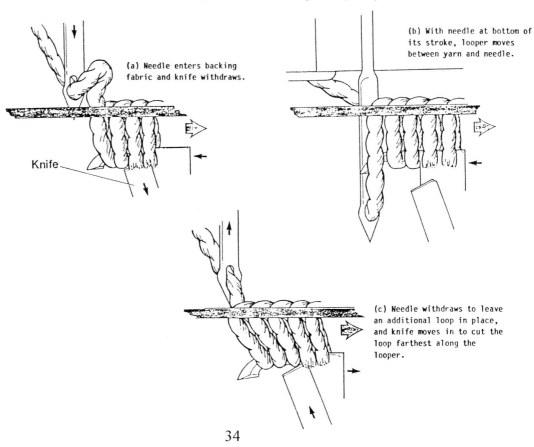

(a) Needle enters backing fabric and knife withdraws.

(b) With needle at bottom of its stroke, looper moves between yarn and needle.

Knife

(c) Needle withdraws to leave an additional loop in place, and knife moves in to cut the loop farthest along the looper.

34

At this point, whether loop or cut pile material is being produced, the fabric is dimensionally unstable, has poor tuft retention and has no flexural rigidity. In this form it is often referred to as *soft cloth*. It is therefore necessary to provide some form of *secondary backing*.

There are various alternatives. Some options include the application of a woven jute or polypropylene material, attached to the pile with a coat of latex; the spreading of a gel or non-gel type foam; or applying a more rigid polymer back-coat such as polyurethane usually applied when it is necessary to provide a carpet with an impervious back as in the case of health care products. The so-called *unitary backed* carpets have no separate secondary backing but a thick coating of latex is applied. Such carpets are only suitable for direct stick installations where the carpet is glued directly to the floor. Also common in the case of tiles, the backing may be a fibrous scrim attached by means of a bituminous coating.

Patterning techniques have improved tremendously in recent years. At first tufted carpets were plain or striped. Then came the development of sliding needle bar arrangements and yarn tensioning techniques, which allowed some limited patterning. Most recently more advanced patterning techniques have allowed the creation of up to six colour patterns not unlike those which may be achieved on a gripper Axminster loom.

BONDING

Bonded carpets, as the name suggests involves 'glueing' the pile to the backing. Indeed, in some cases the carpets have no pile but comprise a fibrous web, impregnated with adhesive.

Perhaps the simplest construction is that of the fibre bonded carpets, also known as needle bonded and needle punch carpets. They are produced by layering fibrous webs from the carding machine and needling through them with barbed needles so that the webs become entangled with one another. They are then impregnated with adhesive to form a boardy like material which serves as a very durable if not especially exciting soft floor covering material.

Another technique involves pressing either coarse yarns, or fibres, into an adhesive which has been spread on some form of support material. (Figure 13) The support material may be a fibre glass non-woven fabric and, in the case of tiles, the adhesive is often a bituminastic product. If coarse yarn is used as the pile it may be pressed into the adhesive with fluted rollers to produce a resultant floor covering that is ribbed in appearance. One product currently available in tile format involves bonding yarns that are presented to the bitumastic adhesive by means of a spool-gripper system in a similar way to that of a woven Axminster.

Cut pile carpets with a U shaped tuft may be produced on the face-to-face principle. Two backing fabrics, (usually jute) are coated with adhesive, and the yarn which makes up the pile is pressed into the adhesive by a *ram* as shown in Figure 14. The two carpets are then slit down the middle using a knife as in the case of face-to-face Wilton production.

Another bonding technique involves flocking using electrostatics to propel short, single fibres into an adhesive coating spread onto a glass fibre matrix supporting scrim. The most familiar of the carpets produced in this way are manufactured from very short (2 - 3 mm long) nylon fibres, often pre-dyed before subsequent screen or roller printing. A very small number of wool carpets are also manufactured by the flocking technique.

Figure 13.   Fluted rollers press carded sliver into adhesive material.

1 doctor blade
2 adhesive
3 support
4 pile yarn

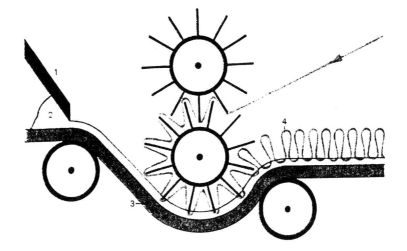

Figure 14.   Bonded carpet produced on the face-to-face principle

1 ram
2 knife
3 backing
4 adhesive
5 pile yarn

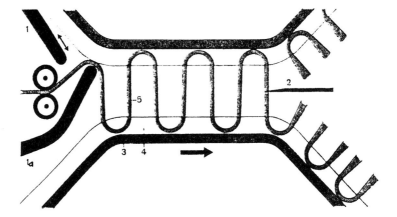

Bonding presents little opportunity for patterning except by printing in some form, with the exception of the spool-gripper method which offers much the same scope as does an Axminster.

The foregoing outline of the manufacture of carpets is intended only as a superficial examination of what is a complex and highly technical process. It is provided in this manual with the primary purpose of giving the carpet inspector the authority, to describe accurately the nature of the floor covering both in terms of its fibre and its constructional characteristics. Furthermore, there are numerous instances when making an inspection, where the manufacturing process has a distinct bearing on the nature of the fault. Examples where this is so will arise in the case histories which follow.

Section Three

Writing a Technical Report

General Rules

There is one important rule that the carpet inspector has to follow, namely that it is not his role to vindicate his client. His responsibility is to establish the truth.

An expert witness in a Court case is known as a *witness of opinion*. He or she is the only individual who is allowed to express an opinion. All other witnesses are expected to state only facts. The job of the expert witness, on the other hand is to enable the Court (ie the judge), to reach a decision on the technicalities of the case. The expert witness's true client therefore is the Court, not the person paying the bill. Every carpet inspector would do well to bear this in mind. Furthermore, every carpet inspector should approach every case as though it is going to end up in Court. Any conclusion drawn should therefore stand the test of "would I be able to say this in Court". If the answer is no, - do not say it.

Do not write a report that says what the client wants to hear. Write a report on what is believed to be the truth. No client is served by false hope or an expert's inaccurate judgement. Otherwise he risks spending thousands on legal fees only to discover that the technical aspects of his case are flawed because the expert has written a report he thought the client *wanted* rather than the report the client *needed*. Besides, judges are not fools. They can tell whether the expert truly believes what he is claiming. Or whether he is simply claiming it to suit the case of his client.[1]

The expert should look upon himself as a kind of 'technical lawyer'. Someone who advises whether the case should go forward on *technical* grounds just as the lawyer decides whether it may be brought on legal grounds. In this way the client can balance his legal advice and the technical advice as to whether or not to proceed.

Of course, most inspections do not go to Court. But some do. That is why the mind set of *probable* Court action should be adopted.

In simple terms the amount of detail in the report will of necessity be determined by the value of the carpet and the amount that the client is prepared to pay. For example some carpet manufacturers are expecting a cheap inspection and in order to satisfy this requirement, the inspector can do no more than complete a *pro forma* inspection report which comprises a few short statements and a rough sketch. Those examples which follow in Section Four are clearly not of this type as this manual is intended primarily to illustrate more comprehensive aspects of report writing. Such reports might reasonably be segmented into four sections:

❑   An introduction which describes the background to the claim
❑   A general description of the fault
❑   The results of any work that has been done off site to assist
       interpretation and therefore help to establish possible causes of the
       fault
❑   General conclusions which firmly state (wherever possible) where the
       blame should lie

For reasons of fluidity these segments may run together in sequence through the report rather than being flagged up by separate subheadings. Nevertheless they will all be there in this

---

[1] See *The Case of the Biased Boffin*

sequence throughout the body of the report. Let us consider the segments in a little more detail:

INTRODUCTION

The introduction states the general background that led to the complaint in the first instance and reviews any actions that may have been undertaken to date. For example a report may already have been submitted by an inspector working for another party; an offer of some financial settlement may have been made and rejected.

Everything that is written in this section of the report could have been written even if the inspector had not been on-site. It is the 'story so far' as told to the inspector by the client. Indeed, aspects may well be contradicted when the inspector gets on site, but at this point the purpose of the introduction is to outline what is understood to be the case. This part of the report therefore serves several purposes:

- It demonstrates that the inspector has understood the information presented to him by his client.
- It gives a concise summary for the benefit of a third party (a judge or lawyer for example) who is new to the story.
- It provides a framework of 'facts' that may be disputed if the tenor of the report is likely to be one of contradiction. In this respect the introduction is actually written with the benefit of hindsight. In other words, at the time of writing the introduction, the inspector has probably decided what conclusions are likely to be drawn. Thus, the introduction will be sure to include any relevant background information that is germane to any of the conclusions which are subsequently drawn.

DESCRIPTION OF THE FAULT

If the inspection is being carried out on behalf of the carpet manufacturer it is likely that he (the carpet manufacturer) has not seen it. Certainly if litigation is involved the legal experts will not have seen it. The inspector is therefore the eyes, and sometimes the ears of the client.

There are a number of features which need to be described:

- The environment and, if there is likely to be any doubt, the typical usage of the carpet. For example a house may be occupied by an elderly couple living alone, or by a family of five with two cats; a commercial premises may have no entrance mat; or there may be large numbers of people wheeling suitcases over the carpet as may be the case in a hotel for instance.
- Precisely how the fault is manifest.
- If the claims being made by the complainant are visible to the inspector and whether these claims differ appreciably from the scenario described in the introduction to the report.

- The area of carpet that is involved. Whether the entire carpet affected by the fault or just a small portion. Whether repair is feasible.

Often, and if the value of the inspection justifies it, the fault may be illustrated by photographs. In these instances the presentation of the report will be enhanced if the photographs can be incorporated into the body of the text rather than submitted loosely with the report. A line diagram of the site may also be useful for illustrative purposes.

In the context of illustration, the report will be considerably improved if it is prepared using a word processor with a computer generated line drawing.

At this stage, the inspector will be sure to draw attention to any specific aspects of the on site inspection that he will be using to form the final conclusions. He will also decide at this point whether to obtain a sample for off-site testing, the results of which are discussed in the next section of the report

SUPPORTING TECHNICAL DATA

It is not unusual, especially in the more complicated cases, for it to be necessary to conduct some work off site.

This work may be undertaken by the inspector himself, or samples may be sent off to an independent laboratory for specialist testing. In such cases, whichever route is followed, it is this testing which provides the real basis upon which the final conclusions may be drawn. It is important therefore that the report provides as much detail as possible, quoting which test methods have been used and whether or not they are recognised national or international standard methods. Clearly, the more authoritative the test method, the greater the amount of credence that may be placed upon the results.

CONCLUSIONS

The conclusions should be saved until last rather than scattered throughout the report. (In a long report they may well be the first section to be read). They should be succinct and state clearly where, in opinion of the inspector, the fault lies.

Section Four

Case Studies

THE CASE OF THE SPORADIC SPOTS

Black spots were occuring over the surface of the carpet. The carpet was relatively new and the spots were not visible when it was first installed. As time went by they became more numerous, noticed first of all in the traffic lanes but in due course becoming visible elsewhere over the entire surface of the carpet. The spots were very small but, because the carpet was pink, they were quite noticeable. (Plate I)

EXAMINATION	NOTES
Simple visual examination with the naked eye suggested that the spot was confined to a single tuft.	
Closer examination under low power magnification *confirmed* that the spot was indeed confined to a single tuft.	An ordinary magnifying glass is all that is required although a textile technologists' *piece glass* is a most useful tool for a carpet inspector to have in is kit.[1]
	It is important to establish whether the spot is confined to a single tuft or is spread over several yarns. An inference can be drawn at once. If the spot affects several tufts it is likely to have occurred after manufacture. However, if it appears confined to a single tuft then it is quite likely that the staining occurred in yarn form. In other words it must have occurred *before* or *during* carpet manufacture rather than after it.
Next the tuft was removed from the carpet by trimming at the level of the backing.	The carpet was tufted. If it had been an Axminster, the entire tuft would have been pulled out using a pair of tweezers. In the case of some tufteds and some Wiltons however, it is usually easier to remove the tuft by trimming.
Further examination of the tuft after removal from the carpet showed that the contamination was confined to one singles component of the two fold yarn.	In other words the carpet yarn was a two-ply yarn but only one ply was contaminated. **This is a very important observation because it means that the contamination has almost certainly arisen during or after spinning of the singles yarn and certainly before *folding* to produce the resultant two-ply yarn.** The information is most important to the manufacturer of the carpet because it helps to establish where the responsibility lies.

[1]Available from James H Heal and Sons Halifax UK

EXAMINATION

An examination of fibres from the affected tuft was carried out under higher magnification and photomicrographs of the image are shown in Plates II and III

From this it will be seen that there is an agglomeration of soil adhering to several of the fibres. Clearly, for soil to adhere in this way there must be some sticky residue on the fibres to which it is able to adhere.

There are thus two clues, obtained by simple observation, which enable the cause to be deduced and an explanation to be given in the report.

Firstly, it is evident that the singles component of the two fold yarn has been contaminated with some form of greasy substance, either during spinning, or before folding (to make a two ply yarn).

Secondly, higher magnification confirms that during use, soil trafficked in under foot has adhered to the sticky areas causing the black spots to appear.

These have appeared gradually since different areas of the carpet are exposed to different amounts of foot traffic. Obviously it is the traffic lanes which reveal the fault first.

The remedy is simple. At such low levels of contamination, cleaning easily removes the oil and the fault is unlikely to reappear.

NOTES

In many investigations of this type the next step is to establish the pH of the affected area. In the present instance it is better to extend the microscopical examination

Every carpet inspector should have an optical microscope. They are not expensive. One which is adequate for the task will cost around £100 - £150. The cost of a typical inspection.

"Elementary my dear Watson"

"No. Sedimentary my dear Holmes."

FLOOR INSPECTION SERVICES LTD
Chorlton cum Hardy

31 August 199x

ABC Carpet Supplies
Somewhere in England

Dear Sirs[1]

Examination of carpet from Rose Cottage, Flowery Fields, Kent[2]

We[3] have now completed our examination of the carpet samples which you submitted, subject of a complaint that faint black marks are appearing in numerous places.[4]

Examination under low power magnification revealed that the marks are intimately associated with one singles component of the two fold yarn. Examination under higher magnification showed that in each case a deposit is present across a bundle of fibres within the singles yarn. In appearance this deposit is typical of oily or greasy contamination to which fine particles of soil have become attached.

Based on this evidence, it is our opinion that the fault has occurred on the yarn either during spinning or after spinning but before folding. This has probably happened as the result of contamination with some colourless oily substance.

The marks are appearing as ordinary household dust particles or deposits from the soles of shoes begin to adhere to this sticky residue. The soil is tenaciously attached to the fibre by the mechanism known as *oil bonding*. Ordinary vacuuming will not overcome such forces of adhesion.

The fault is clearly a manufacturing defect[5] although it is likely that it can be corrected by spotting and cleaning.[6]

Yours faithfully,

S Holmes

---

[1] The job is small enough and simple enough to report in letter format. However, you should adopt the more formal style of writing to the company rather than an individual.
[2] Begin the report with a heading that defines the specimen that is being examined.
[3] Because a formal style has been adopted the report is not your private opinion, it is that of your company for whom you are the spokesperson.
[4] When the report is presented in the form of a letter, try to define the problem in the first paragraph.
[5] Do not prevaricate if you know the answer.
[6] Try to end on a constructive note.

THE CASE OF THE BICOMPONENT BLUNDER

Grey carpet tiles in the office of a city stockbroker were becoming yellow in all traffic lanes and beneath castor chairs. The stockbroker complained to the carpet manufacturer who had tests carried out which showed that the cleaning contractor was cleaning the carpets using a strongly alkaline shampoo. The contractor denied that this was the case and claimed instead that the carpet tiles were faulty.

EXAMINATION	NOTES
The carpet in question was a loop pile tile which was essentially grey in shade but contained effect threads which were coloured rust yellow, gold and green. Upon inspection it was clear that severe yellowing was occurring in all traffic lanes. The yellowing was worst of all beneath castor chairs. Two tiles from an uncleaned area and two from a discoloured area were uplifted for testing.	Always ensure that samples of 'normal' and 'faulty' material are obtained for testing wherever possible.
In the laboratory examination it was obvious that in the case of the faulty tiles there was a tendency for the coloured effect yarns to stand proud of the surface. This was particularly noticeable if the tiles were viewed under conditions of incident lighting.	Use as many of the senses as possible. In the present instance the sense of touch suggested this tendency for the yarn to stand proud. Close visual examination confirmed that this was indeed the case.
	The angle of illumination is important in the viewing of textile complaints. It may be necessary to view under direct illumination, under incident light or even with light shining through the product in some circumtances.
pH tests revealed that the unused specimen was neutral in pH and the cleaned specimen was slightly acidic. This evidence tended to contradict that of the manufacturer's expert who claimed that alkaline cleaning was the cause of the problem.	
The owner of the carpet provided information from the manufacturer to show that the pile was a blend of 50% nylon and 50% polypropylene.	
With this in mind a specimen of the unaffected tile was treated in boiling xylene to remove the polyolefin component whilst another was treated in m-cresol to remove the nylon. These samples are shown in Plate IV.[1]	See *Diagnostic Techniques for the Identification of Carpet Complaints* with regard to the solubility of different fibres. Take care xylene is inflammable and cresol is corrosive to human tissue and is poisonous.

---

[1] In Plate IV, the two treated specimens are shown resting on top of a new and an used tile which have been placed side by side. The specimen showing the nylon residue (multicoloured) has been placed upon the used tile and the specimen showing the polypropylene residue (grey) has been placed upon a new tile. This has been done to illustrate the difference in colours of the new and used tiles as well as showing the difference in colour of the residues.

EXAMINATION

Following this procedure it was discovered that *all* of the coloured effect yarns were nylon, whilst all of the grey background yarns were polyolefin.

Polyolefin (ie polypropylene) has a poor resistance to compression. Much worse than that of nylon. It is thus reasonable to assume that in use the grey polyolefin yarns were compressing preferrentially, leaving the coloured nylon yarns, which were mainly yellow in shade, to stand proud on the surface. The result was a gradual shift in shade from a product that was essentially grey in appearance to one that appeared to be yellow. This shift in shade obviously could be expected to be worst in the areas of heaviest wear which was the case in all traffic lanes, and especially beneath castor chairs.

One final test was carried out to demonstrate to the client that the carpet construction was fundamentally flawed. Specimens of the unused carpet were subjected to 12000 revolutions on a Hexapod Tumbler Tester in accordance with British Standard BS 6659. The carpet became yellower during the course of this test as the polypropylene component of the carpet became preferrentially flattened.

NOTES

There can be no doubt that this is a manufacturing fault. The construction of a pile where some yarns are made from 100% of one type of fibre whilst others are made from 100% of another type of fibre, (especially when the performance of the two types of fibre can be expected to be so different), is fundamentally unsound. If a blend of 50% of each of two different fibre types is desired, then *every pile yarn* that makes up the carpet should be blended in those proportions.

FLOOR INSPECTION SERVICES LTD
Chorlton cum Hardy

11 June 199x

Acme Cleaners Ltd
North of Watford

Dear Sirs

Examination of carpet at the offices of Bermondsey Brokers Ltd London EC2

We refer to our visit to the above premises to examine the carpets subject of a complaint of yellowing after cleaning.

The carpet in question is essentially grey in shade but is coloured with effect threads in rust, yellow, gold and green amongst others. Upon inspection it was clear that it is the traffic lanes that are yellowing although areas beneath castor chairs are even more severely affected. A report from the manufacturer suggested that the effect has been caused by cleaning under alkaline conditions.

Two tiles from an uncleaned area and two from a damaged area were uplifted for testing. In the laboratory it quickly became clear that in the faulty tiles there was a tendency for the coloured effect threads to stand proud of the surface. This was particularly noticeable if the pile was viewed under conditions of incident lighting.

Solubility tests revealed that the yarns consisted of either nylon fibres or polyolefin fibres. With this in mind, a specimen of the unaffected tile was treated in boiling xylene to remove the polyolefin component whilst another was treated in m-cresol to remove the nylon component. As a result of this procedure it was discovered that the effect yarns were all 100% nylon whilst the grey background yarns were 100% polyolefin.

A sample of the unaffected carpet was subjected to 12000 cycles in a Hexapod Tumbler Tester. This instrument is used to assess the appearance retention characteristics of carpets. The specimen became yellower as a result of this treatment. Additionally, the pH of aqueous extracts of the used and unused specimens was determined. The unused specimen was almost neutral and the used was very slightly acidic. (pH6).

We have no doubt what has caused the unacceptable appearance. Polyolefin fibre has poor ability to recover from compression. Nylon has greater ability. Thus, during use, the grey polyolefin fibre is compressing preferentially leaving the coloured nylon yarns to predominate on the surface thereby altering the perceived colour of the carpet. The fact that the effect is even more severe under the castor chairs only serves to substantiate this opinion, as indeed does the Hexapod test.

Cleaning is not the cause of the changes that have occurred. Rather it is the basic construction of the carpet face fabric that is fundamentally unsound.

Yours faithfully,

THE CASE OF THE BURGUNDY BLEEDER

A carpet cleaner, faced with the task of cleaning a wool rich Axminster carpet, laid in the reception lobby and banqueting areas of a small privately owned provincial hotel, noticed that wherever there had been a drinks spillage, the burgundy coloured yarn in the pattern, had bled.

Aware that most drinks are neutral or even acidic in character he was careful to pretest an area before commencing the work.

Not only did the colour run in the presence of his normal (neutral) cleaning agent, but in subsequent tests first with tap water alone, and then even using a product intended for acid rinsing, the same phenomenon occurred.

Anxious to keep a good customer, the cleaner explained to his client that the carpet must be faulty and an independent inspection was arranged.

FLOOR INSPECTION SERVICES LTD
Chorlton cum Hardy

29 February, 199x

The Inn of the Sixth Happiness
Shangrila
Nowhere near Watford

Dear Ms Bergman[1]

Examination of carpet at the Inn of the Sixth Happiness

I[2] refer to my visit to your hotel to examine the carpets laid throughout the reception area and banqueting suite. The carpet is a wool rich Axminster in beige, green, blue and burgundy shades and it is clear that where drinks spillages have occurred, the burgundy yarn is bleeding into the adjacent beige. Your carpet cleaner has also confirmed that even under acidic conditions (conditions under which wool dyes are usually quite stable), the dye is still fugitive.

I have now carried out laboratory tests on the off-cut which you provided. In particular I removed tufts of burgundy coloured yarn and tested the colour fastness of this yarn in accordance with British Standard 1006:1990 *Methods of test for the colour fastness of textiles and leather.*[3] The change of shade of the specimen, and the staining of white wool and white cotton was assessed using standard grey scales as follows:

Fastness rating

Change of shade	5
Staining of white wool	1-2
Staining of white cotton	2-3

In the table, 5 represents no change of shade or staining and 1 represents severe change of shade or staining.[4]

These values fall below commercially acceptable tolerances and you therefore have a valid claim against the supplier of your carpet.

Yours sincerely,

H Poirot

---

[1] Sometimes a less formal approach may be taken. Remember this is a small, privately owned provincial hotel and the report, though still intended for possible use in Court, is written in a more friendly, advisory style.

[2] Thus, the first person singular is used.

[3] Wherever possible conduct tests in accordance with national standards. Always quote the number and title.

[4] A result as low as 1-2 is clearly quite unacceptable. 2-3 is also poor. (See Plate V)

THE CASE OF THE MANIC MECHANIC

An 80% wool / 20% nylon Axminster carpet had completely disintegrated (See Plate VI). The carpet was installed in the living room of a house where the son was a motorcycle enthusiast

EXAMINATION	NOTES
	Carpets in such a distressed state as this are typical of the effects of damage to the backing. This damage may be the result of mildew for example. Or it may be the result of acid damage. The scenario (son who is a motorcycle enthusiast) immediately calls to mind the possibility of acid damage from batteries (which contain sulphuric acid). This is the first aspect to check. Polypropylene is unaffected by acids.
Visual examination revealed that the backing was jute.	If your instinct about acid damage is correct, the backing has to be jute.
Microscopical examination showed that the wool fibres were unaffected. However the nylon was severely degraded.	Wool is unaffected by acid. Nylon is dissolved.
pH tests were carried out on aqueous extracts of normal and degraded carpet. The normal carpet was found to be approximately pH 6. The degraded carpet however had a pH of less than 2. Tests for the presence of sulphate ions were carried out on the aqueous extracts. The normal carpet gave negative results whilst the damaged carpet gave strongly positive results. (See Plate VII).[1]	Test methods for obtaining aqueous extracts and for confirming the presence of sulphate ions are given in *Diagnostic Techniques for the Identification of Carpet Complaints*.

Always remember to test normal carpet as well as faulty carpet. |
| The highly acidic pH and the presence of an abundance of sulphate ions is highly indicative of damage by sulphuric acid. In a domestic installation the most common source of sulphuric acid is car battery acid. | If the pile had been 100% nylon on a jute backing, both pile and backing would have been affected. If however the pile was nylon on a polypropylene backing only the pile yarn would have been affected. These circumstantial clues are as easy to corroborate with pH tests and tests for sulphate on nylon as they are on wool or wool rich blends. If the carpet had been polypropylene pile on a polypropylene backing the battery acid would have had no significant effect.

Similar breakdown will occur in the case of hydrochloric acid, nitric acid and phosphoric acid. |

[1] In the illustration the white precipitate shows the presence of sulphate in the faulty and the red pH shows that the faulty extract is highly acidic. (The other tubes are extracts from the normal carpet)

THE CASE OF THE LITIGIOUS LAWYER

A resort hotel in the United States had purchased some 2500 square metres of an 80% wool / 20% nylon Axminster carpet. Shortly after installation they complained that tufts were being lost; that the carpets were unravelling along the seams; and that colour fastness to crocking (rubbing) was below acceptable tolerances.

Tests carried out by an American laboratory on behalf of the hotel determined that the tuft bind was a mere 10 oz (280 g) and that the carpet therefore failed to meet the minimum tuft bind requirements of HUD (Department of Housing and Development) standards which demand some 4.5 lb (2 Kg); and that the colour fastness to crocking was below acceptable tolerances.

In contrast an inspection carried out on behalf of the manufacturer by a local inspection service concluded that tufts were only being lost at seamed areas and 'other stress points' and that the condition had resulted only from overwetting of the carpet. The local inspector also reported that in 'manual tests' the tuft bind appeared to meet the minimum requirement of 4.5 lbs as demanded in the HUD standard.

These conclusions were totally rejected by the hotel not least because at the time of the local inspection no wet cleaning had been undertaken. Furthermore the laboratory tests showed that the 'manual' tests were wrong.

The complainant had retained the services of a lawyer who was present at the inspection and who seemed intent throughout on trying to intimidate the inspector with tales of multimillion dollar law suits and threats to place the matter before a jury. When asked what his client required for an out-of-Court settlement, he replied ' a new carpet at significantly less than half cost price!'

EXAMINATION

Two days before the inspection Hurricane Bob visited the premises and settled the dispute in relation to one of the five areas of carpet involved (See Plate VIII). Because of the hurricane another of the carpets had been totally submerged in sea water and was being dried out with air movers thereby preventing any satisfactory examination from being made. However several other areas were able to be inspected, most notably the ballroom where the principal complaint of tuft loss had occurred.

There was clear evidence of tuft loss. However, this tuft loss always occurred at a seam. The installer who was present on site at the time of the inspection indicated that about 50% of the seams had been sewn and the remainder were taped and latexed. Furthermore tuft loss only occurred at those seams where the carpet had been cut across the warp (to make a border effect). Close inspection revealed that there had been no attempt to seal these raw seams.

Other examples of poor installation techniques were found in different rooms. In particular large gaps between the gripper and the wall were found. Such large gaps were clearly contrary to the techniques laid down in the industry recommended Code of Practice.

As for the allegations of poor colour fastness these related to a trial that had been undertaken by the local representative of a cleaning product manufacturer. He had cleaned a small area of the carpet using his normal product and bleeding had occurred. Aqueous extracts taken from this portion of carpet showed that the pile was strongly alkaline in this area. Adjacent, uncleaned areas were neutral. Additionally it was quite obvious that those carpets which had been totally submerged by sea water following the hurricane showed no evidence of colour bleeding.

Off-cuts of new, unused carpet were taken for laboratory testing. Colour fastness to rubbing (which was not a particularly relevant test but was one of those carried out by the customer's laboratory) and colour fastness to water both showed that the performance of all of the carpets was excellent.

Colour fastness to wet rubbing gave results of at least *4* for each of the four patterns, and a result of *4-5* for dry rubbing. Colour fastness to water gave results of *5* for change of shade and no worse than *4* for staining of white wool and white cotton.

[In both tests 1 represents severe change and 5 represents no change]

Tuft withdrawal tests showed strengths ranging from 8.2 to 15.8 Newtons (1.8 to 3.4 lb). These results are especially good for Axminster carpets where much lower values are acceptable. The US HUD standard applies to tufted carpets where values of 4.5 lb are possible. Such a requirement is totally unrealistic for an Axminster carpet.

The report of the examination is shown almost in its entirety on the following pages. It refers to the US installation standard but this does not differ significantly in its requirements from that of the British Standard Code of Practice BS 5325:1996

After the hotel had received the report the manufacturer heard nothing more from the litigious lawyer who until then had been threatening hellfire and damnation.

Examination of carpets at the Holly Shoreline Hotel[1]

Introduction[2]

A dispute has arisen between the Holly Group and Agreeable Axminsters Inc concerning the supply of carpets to the Holly Shoreline Resort and Conference Center.

Holly Group claim that the carpets are defective and should be replaced after only two years in use. In particular they claim:

1. That the carpets are 'unravelling' along several of the seams.
2. That tufts are being lost even where no seam is involved.
3. That the colour fastness to crocking[3] is below acceptable tolerances which prevents the carpets from being cleaned properly.

In order to support their claim, Holly submitted certain specimens to Independent Carpet Testing Labs Inc in November 199x. They determined tuft bind, colour fastness to crocking, colour fastness to light, and colour fastness to water. On the strength of their results lawyers Beauchamp, Cholmondley and Smythe acting on behalf of Holly, further claimed:

4. That one tested specimen had a tuft bind of only 10 oz. (280 g).
5. That the laboratory had concluded that the carpet fails to meet minimum standards as laid down by the Department of Housing and Urban Development (HUD).
6. That the colour fastness of the carpets is inadequate.

It is understood that Agreeable Axminsters have not seen the ICTL reports in which these last two allegations are made.

In April, before ICTL's involvement, Agreeable Axminsters retained Clouzot's Inspection Services Inc. to examine the installation. The inspector, Clouzot himself, confirmed that severe unravelling (*sic*) had indeed occurred.[4] He also observed that this condition 'is contained (*sic*) only to the seamed areas of the carpet as well as other stress points'. Overwetting was blamed[5].

Additionally the report observed:

---

[1] A simple letter is not acceptable for an investigation of this type. Litigation is a serious possibility and the report might well be used in Court. A professional presentation will go a long way towards convincing the judge that you are a competent expert.
[2] The introduction sets the scene for someone reading the report for the first time eg the Judge
[3] Rubbing
[4] It is doubtful whether a competent inspector would ever use the term 'unravelling' in connection with a woven carpet and use of this word by a so called expert immediately rings warning bells about the usefulness of his report.
[5] Clouzot presumed this overwetting occurred during cleaning. Unfortunately he failed to establish that wet cleaning had never been undertaken.

1. That the carpets appeared to have been sealed at the edges before making any seams.

2. That in manual tests (*sic*) tuft bind appears 'to meet or exceed the minimum amount of 4.5 lbs'[6]

Holly Group have rejected the report of Clouzot's Inspection Services Inc.

Against this background a second inspection was undertaken by Cleaning Research International Ltd.[7]

In Situ Examination

An on site inspection was undertaken on 23 June 199x. Present at the meeting were.......[8]

In the preliminary discussions before the inspection took place some additional information was obtained.[9]

In May 198x carpets in four designs were laid in the following areas: Dining Room, Tidal Lounge, Seashore Bar, Ballroom, Main Corridor, Piano Bar, Lower Lobby, Lobby and Conference Lobby. These areas are identified on the plan shown in Appendix I[10].

Some four or five months later a claim of unravelling at the seams was identified.[11]

Mr [Facilities Manager] called the installer back to the site, expressing the view that the seaming was at fault. The installer however suggested that the carpet was substandard.[12] This opinion was reinforced when, it is claimed, tuft loss (unravelling) was observed in the dining room in an area not adjacent to any seaming.

The conclusions drawn by the inspector, Clouzot, were totally rejected on the grounds that the carpet had not been wet cleaned.

Additional information obtained during this discussion revealed the following:

1. A cleaning trial had been conducted by Cowboy Colin's Carpet Cleaning Company of Colorado which had caused colour bleeding.

---

[6] Agreeable Axminsters did themselves no favours in retaining the services of Clouzot. Even the least technically qualified (ie the lawyer) must realise that by gripping a tuft with a pair of tweezers and pulling, it is impossible to estimate the tuft withdrawal force manually.

[7] This completes the introduction and brings forth any salient features which may either be supported or demolished in the report which follows.

[8] List the names of the participants

[9] The text which follows could alternatively have been included in the introduction as part of the scene setting. In the present instance it is included as part of the on site inspection report because it was during discussions with the various parties, and especially the litigious lawyer, that much of this information was first revealed.

[10] A plan is useful to assist the Judge in his comprehension of the scale of the claim.

[11] Now we know the origin of Clouzot's terminology. He has simply used that of the claimant.

[12] To quote Mandy Rice-Davies, - 'he would, wouldn't he?'

2.   Irresponsible Ian (the incompetent installer from Iowa) indicated that 50% of the seams were hand sewn and the remainder were taped and latexed. He also indicated that wool carpets cannot be wet cleaned and should only be cleaned by absorbent compound type cleaners![13]

On the day of the inspection the complex was suffering the aftermath of Hurricane Bob which had passed through the resort a few days previously. This hurricane had caused severe damage to the Tidal Lounge such that all of the windows had been blown in, and the carpet had been saturated with sand, sea water and glass and thrown into heaps on the floor. (Plate VII). The carpet and padding[14] in the Seashore Bar, the Dining Room and part of the Ballroom were saturated with sea water. Power had only been restored that morning with the consequence that drying of the wet carpets had only just commenced. Carpets in the Lobby, Piano Bar, and Conference Lobby were essentially unaffected by the hurricane.

During the course of the *in situ*[15] examination the following observations were made.

1.   Four different patterns were supplied in the manufacturer's *Planet Suite* quality. These were all 9 row Axminsters in 80% wool / 20% nylon. Table 1 shows the areas in which each pattern was laid together with the amount of carpet involved.[16]

Table 1.   Details of carpet supplied[17]
....

2.   In the Ballroom, there was evidence that some loss of tufts had occurred. Fraying of the weft was also evident in some instances. In every case this breakdown was coincident with a seam.[18]

Furthermore, only seams which were made by cutting across the warp were involved.[19] (the Ballroom carpet was installed in the currently fashionable border/area rug effect configuration.

---

[13] Because of the lack of experience of wool carpets in the United States this type of misunderstanding is not uncommon.

[14] Underlay

[15] Some believe that it is a nice touch to place foreign words and phrases in italics.

[16] Not reproduced in this specimen report for reasons of space but important information that should be included in the report to help quantify the scope of the claim.

[17] Tables, diagrams and figures should always be numbered and bear a title. When the report is typed it may be necessary, for reasons of layout to displace the position of the table. By giving it a heading you avoid any ambiguity in relating the information contained in the table to the relevant part of your report.

[18] An important point this. There have been suggestions that tufts were coming out all over the place. Even Clouzot who was supposed to be on our side reported a loss of tufts at 'stress points'. (Whatever that may mean).

[19] An even more important point this, moving towards the conclusion that faulty installation is involved. Remember, by the time you write the report you have already formed your opinion, The report should therefore be set out in such a way as to lead the reader to reach the same opinion which you have reached as though he is stumbling upon the reason for the complaint by himself.

This means that although some seams have been made selvedge to selvedge others involved cutting across the direction of manufacture. This cutting inevitably produces a rough unfinished edge).

Examination of the cut edges revealed that the correct installation practice had been ignored in two ways:

> a.   Raw edges were not frayed back, tucked under, and latexed to make good the damage done by the cutting to the integrity of the construction.

> b.   No seam sealer was applied to the raw edge.

The *Carpet and Rug Institute* publication *Standard for Installation of Textile Floor Covering Materials* (CRI 104 - 1988 Dalton, Georgia) states:

'10.4.2.   Trim all edges that are to be used for seaming at least one inch on each side.'

'10.5   **Edge securing** - Once the edges are trimmed, an appropriate seam sealer must be applied to both edges. Improper sealed edges are the main problem with seam failures'[20]

Plates A and B illustrate the inadequacy of the seaming technique.[21] [22] This was pointed out to Mr [owner], Mr [installer] and Mr [litigious lawyer] at the time. There was no evidence of tuft loss anywhere else in the Ballroom except along similar seams. Despite being totally immersed in sea water, no colour migration was apparent in any of the designs.[23] In one section of the leaf design however a shade change was evident. It was reported that this was where the cleaning trial had been undertaken by Messrs [Cowboy Colin]. This had prompted the claim that the carpet could not be cleaned. The pH of an aqueous extract taken from this area of carpet was found to be highly alkaline (Approximately 9.5). An unaffected area was slightly acidic.[24]

> 3.   Except for the flooding, there was no obvious evidence of any damage in the carpet installed in the Seashore Bar and the complainant was unable to point any out when challenged to do so. Despite the fact that this carpet had been left for several days, no colour migration had occurred. This infers that the water fastness of the carpet is extremely good.

---

[20] Show that you are familiar with the standard. Irresponsible Ian the Installer obviously isn't. Quote standards every time you have an opportunity to do so. even if the standard is only a Code of Practice, it represents 'best technique' and as such should be followed by all who claim to be professionals.

[21] A good time to illustrate your observations with photographic evidence 'for the Judge'. Plate IX here shows one of the actual photographs from the report.

[22] The sentence is a positive one that brooks no fear of contradiction. As you move through towards your conclusion more and more positive statements that dare the opposition to challenge you should be made. You should aim to undermine their resolve with your confidence.

[23] Hurricane Bob did the manufacturer a big favour. Total immersion in sea water is far more aggressive than any laboratory test that might be devised. The fact that the carpet withstood this gross mistreatment must have sewn seeds of doubt in the minds of the complainants.

[24] Fortunately the cleaned area of carpet was in a part that had not been submerged.

This carpet was not laid in the border/rug effect configuration. Nevertheless there was evidence of bad installation technique. Plate C illustrates the position of the tackless strip[25] relative to the wall. It has been placed several inches from the wall. The Carpet and Rug Institute standard (*op. cit.*) requires:

'10.2.1.   **Installation of Tackless Strip** - The installation procedure for tackless strip shall be as follows: ....

        B.   Determine the proper gully, slightly less than the thickness of the carpet but not to exceed 3/8 inch'[26]

        4.   Except for the flooding, there was no obvious evidence of any damage in the carpet installed in the small leaf design and the complainant was unable to point any out when challenged to do so. Despite the fact that this carpet had been left for several days, no colour migration had occurred. This infers that the water fastness of this carpet is also extremely good.[27]

        5.   There was no evidence of any fault in the carpet in the Teal Blue shade except at seams in the Ballroom. No problem was pointed out anywhere else with respect to this carpet.

        6.   It was alleged that tuft loss occurred away from a seam in the Tidal Lounge carpet. Unfortunately, this carpet had been damaged by the hurricane to such an extent that it was impossible to check the validity of this claim. There was evidence that seams had not been sealed in this room either. (Plate D).[28]

        7.   It was impossible to confirm the installer's claim that 50% of the seams were hand sewn. None were seen at the time of the inspection but it is true to say that not every seam was examined.

Laboratory Testing

Four small samples, one in each pattern were submitted for testing. Tuft withdrawal force was determined in accordance with British Standard 5229:1975. (This standard is very similar to ASTM D 1335)[29] The results are shown in Table 2.[30] Colour fastness to rubbing was determined in accordance with British Standard BS1006:1990. (This standard is similar to AATCC Test Method 165 - Colour Fastness to Crocking). These results are shown in Table 3.[31]

---

[25] Gripper

[26] Another nail in the installer's coffin.

[27] There is no harm in repeating the same point almost verbatim. The inference is to convey a sense of 'isn't this tedious; yet another carpet that has nothing wrong with it.'

[28] Despite the carpet being destroyed it was still possible to find unfinished seams which were photographed and included in the report.

[29] The appropriate American Standard

[30] Not reproduced here but the four specimens ranged from 1.8 to 3.4 lbs which, as we have observed earlier is extremely good for Axminster carpets.

[31] Again the results are not shown here but were not less than 4. (5 is excellent; 1 very poor).

mined in accordance with British Standard BS1006:1990. (This standard is similar to AATCC Test Method 165 - Colour Fastness to Crocking). These results are shown in Table 3.[31]

Table 2. Tuft Withdrawal characteristics of four carpets

………

Table 3. Colour fastness to rubbing of four carpets

……..

Conclusions

The claim against Agreeable Axminsters Inc is based upon on-site performance supported by laboratory test results. Let us then consider the results obtained by Independent Carpet Testing Labs Inc. For convenience they are reproduced in Tables 4 and 5.[32]

Table 4 etc.
Table 5 etc.

Water fastness results obtained by ICTL show the performance in this respect to be excellent.

Let us then consider the claim in some detail. It falls into two parts:

1.   Tuft loss is occurring

Tuft loss is indeed occurring.[33]

During the examination however the only examples where this was taking place was at seams. This is clearly the result of poor seaming technique and is thus an installation fault. the installer has not followed the guidelines laid down by the authoritative Carpet and Rug Institute, and Holly Group have suffered the consequences.

There are no other examples of tuft loss.

It is claimed that the Tidal Lounge carpet exhibited tuft loss at places other than seams. Unfortunately, because of the hurricane these examples could not be found. However the carpet in the Tidal Lounge is the same as that in the Ballroom which is perfectly satisfactory except at seams. It is reasonable to assume therefore that the reported tuft loss was a consequence of some localised trauma.[34]

---

[31] Again the results are not shown here but were not less than 4. (5 is excellent; 1 very poor).
[32] ICTL's tuft withdrawal results ranged from 1.2 lb (5.4N) to 3.3 lb (15N). It is not clear where the oft quoted figure of 10 oz came from. Their colour fastness to 'crocking' figures ranged from 3 - 4 to 4 - 5 on new material and 2 - 3 on so-called 'existing' material whatever that might be.
[33] If something is plain for all to see do not be frightened of stating it boldly in the report. You are about to begin to explain why.
[34] A Judge would accept this logic. The carpet was totally written off anyway, so of no real interest in any subsequent litigation.

The tuft withdrawal results obtained both by ICTL and ourselves are well within commercially acceptable tolerances for Axminster carpets. Figures as low as 3.0N (0.7 lb) are perfectly acceptable in the UK and Europe and the Canadian Specifications Board Standard (4 - GP - 129 1972) accepts 4.5N (1 lb). In the US, the Wool Bureau[35] permit 3.5 N (0.8 lb) for their certification schemes. The quoted HUD standard is not applicable in this installation (and indeed would be extremely difficult to attain in any conventional Axminster carpet).[36]

2.   The carpets are uncleanable

As far as colour fastness to crocking is concerned the following arguments pertain:

a.   Crocking fastness is not the correct test to assess the cleanability of a carpet. Colour fastness to water or shampoo is far more relevant. In water fastness tests carried out by ICTL the performance was excellent.[37] The evidence on site, after flooding, bears out these results.

b.   There is no evidence on site of dark shades bleeding into light shades, except where the cleaning trial was carried out.

However, there is evidence to show in the cleaning test area that the pile is strongly alkaline. Wool dyes are often unstable in the presence of alkali. A truly professional carpet cleaner will be aware of this fact and choose his chemicals accordingly. Furthermore the manufacturer's own cleaning instructions, supplied with the carpets, clearly advise against the use of alkaline detergents.

In conclusion it should be observed that the report of Clouzot's Inspection Services is severely flawed in three respects:

a.   There is no evidence of shrinkage, which would have been accompanied by changes in the dimensions of patterns and possibly by bowing or skewing. (Neither changes in dimensions nor bowing and skewing were found not to be the case)

b.   It is obvious to all that seams have not been sealed though Clouzot believes that they have.

c.   Tuft bind cannot be determined *in situ* and reference to so-called 'manual tests' must therefore be rejected.

The claim of faulty manufacture is clearly unjustified and should be vigorously defended.

---

[35] Now Wools of New Zealand

[36] The HUD standard was always a red herring, introduced into the argument by someone who clearly did not understand Axminsters. I believe it applies to tufted carpets bought by local authorities for housing projects (akin to Council run homes).

[37] It was also excellent in our tests but it is far better to quote the results from the lab that they chose.

THE CASE OF THE BIASED BOFFIN

An 80% wool / 20 % nylon Axminster carpet was sold to a government department in the United States. Soon after installation, the office manager arranged for a silicone based carpet protector to be applied to the carpet. The application was carried out whilst the office was still in the process of occupation and it was therefore decided, some three weeks later, to treat the carpet again with the same protector to be doubly sure that any carpet previously untreated (because of the obstruction of packing cases etc) would not be missed on the second occasion.

Within three months the carpet was said to have 'uglied out' (as opposed to worn out). One portion was replaced at once with a competitor's product and proceedings were begun against the manufacturer.

The government agency retained the services of an expert witness, (expert in cotton technology) who claimed that the carpet was manufactured from a high proportion of skin wool and was therefore inferior. The issue was further clouded by the fact that pile weight tests carried out in the US differed significantly from tests carried out by the manufacturer in the UK. With this evidence, the customer commenced proceedings for a new carpet at a replacement cost of some $120000.

The manufacturer defended the suit.

THE PLAINTIFF'S CASE

After the appearance of the carpet became unacceptable in use, the Plaintiff arranged for an off-cut to be tested by a reputable carpet testing laboratory. A number of screening tests were carried out after which it was alleged that the pile weight of the carpet as supplied was lower than that given in the manufacturer's specification. This finding led the Plaintiff to conclude that the carpet was substandard, the underweight specification being responsible for the early failure.

Around the same time, it became necessary to replace part of the carpet because attempts to correct errors in the alignment of a decorative insert had resulted in unsightly seams. However, because of their level of dissatisfaction and therefore rather than use attic stock of the existing carpet, the Plaintiff decided to purchase similar carpet from a competitive manufacturer, made to the same specification.

This carpet showed none of the effects of premature ageing as demonstrated by the Defendant's product and reinforced the Plaintiff's view that compensation was appropriate.

When it became clear that the Defendant intended to challenge the claim, the Plaintiff engaged the services of one Dr Brittanica whose encyclopaedic knowledge of cotton technology they felt, made him an emminently suitable expert witness in matters concerning wool/nylon carpets! Dr Brittanica examined fibres from the carpet under the microscope and made two important observations:

    i.   The wool component of the blend contained a very large proportion of pulled wool.[1]

    ii   There were seven different types of nylon in the blend. This suggested that the yarn had been made from reclaimed materials[2] or at the very best, from inferior nylon.

The Plaintiff's case came before the Court some four years after the initial installation. They alleged poor performance on the grounds of substandard material based upon three separate issues:

- Underweight pile
- The use of inferior quality wool
- The use of inferior quality nylon

The Plaintiff's expert occupied the witness box for some four hours during which time he was full of bluster and accusation even to the extent of rejecting evidence by the Defendants about which he clearly had no expertise or understanding.

---

[1] Also known as skin wool, which is wool usually obtained from the carcasses of dead sheep where usually alkaline treatment (but occasionally natural decomposition) allows wool fibres to be 'plucked' from the fleeces rather than shorn. Such fibres, to a trained microscopist have a very characteristic appearance).

[2] Known in the trade as *shoddy*.

The Defendant's case

The Defendant rejected allegations that the carpet pile weight was below specification but argued rather that the shortfall could be accounted for by different practices between the US method of determining pile weight (ie not allowing for regain[3]), and the UK practice of determining pile weight (ie with regain allowances). Clearly, they said, the difference in pile weight could be accounted for in this way. Additionally, during Discovery,[4] it was found that the competitor's decorative insert, used instead of the Defendant supplied attic stock, was also below specification for pile weight. Yet this was a US supplied carpet and so presumably not subject to confusion over test method differences between US and UK practices. Furthermore the Plaintiff claimed that this replacement carpet had performed satisfactorily in end use.

The Defendant also rejected Dr Brittanica's claim that pulled wool had been used in the blend. Not only was the yarn supplier able to confirm that no such material had been used but microscopists skilled in wool recognition also stated categorically that there was no microscopical evidence whatsoever to support the Plaintiff's expert's view. Similar specialists also rejected the claim that reused nylon was present in the blend. They believed that Britannica was seeing variations in filament denier between nylons originating either from different batches or from different suppliers.[5]

Finally, the Defendant was able to produce a series of reports, produced by independent laboratories, which showed that the appearance retention characteristics of the carpet, (as assessed using a Hexapod) and the abrasion characteristics of the carpet, were well within acceptable tolerances.

The defendants claimed instead that the problem was related to the application of the silicone 'protector'. They believed that the stickiness of the product had caused the carpet to loose its ability to recover from compression. Thus, when walked upon, the pile would flatten and not spring back as might normally be expected. This, they argued, would occur early in the life of the carpet, after which no radical changes were likely to occur thereafter, Indeed, examination of the carpet some four years after it was installed, and in comparison with the competitor's carpet also after almost four year's use, revealed that, in terms of appearance, there was now nothing to choose between the two.[6]

---

[3] Standard allowance for moisture content as opposed to oven dry weight

[4] The process whereby the evidence each side intends to use, is shown to the other side.

[5] Given the degree of mixing that takes place in the blending operation and the fact that a spinner may well process many different blends through the same machinery, it is not unusual to find some raw material variation in a yarn arising from fibres left behind from the processing of earlier batches.

[6] During the hearing, the manufacturer's expert also demonstrated that the edges of the carpet which had not been exposed to foot traffic, still had a tendency to feel sticky, even though four years had elapsed since the original application of the silicone protector.

THE JUDGEMENT

The case was heard in the Superior Court of the State of Utopia before His Honour Judge Solomon and continued over a period of four days. Witnesses were heard from both parties.

Firstly, the Plaintiff established the sequence of events leading up to the complaint and a number of experts were called to confirm that the performance of the carpet had indeed been substandard. Next Dr Brittanica proceeded to explain exactly why the carpet was substandard; namely that it was underweight, that it had been made from pulled wool and that inferior nylon was present in the blend. He then stridently expressed his own views about unscrupulous carpet manufacturers and the way that the Defendant in particular was clearly trying to fob off his client with second grade material. Indeed, he became so carried away at one point that the Judge expressed his own view that he would like 'a little less heat and a little more light from the witness'.

The Defendant showed that there were differences between UK and US custom for determining pile weight and defended their position for choosing UK custom. They also showed that the competitor's carpet would equally have failed this particular test yet had performed to the Plaintiff's satisfaction. They then proceeded to dispute the conclusions drawn by Dr Brittanica with respect to the quality of the wool and nylon fibres, challenging his competence as an expert in wool microscopy.

Supported by other test results which showed that their carpet as supplied met acceptable criteria for general performance and appearance retention, they explained to the Court the shortcomings of topical sprays using Silicone based products and attributed the reasons for failure entirely to the decision to treat their carpet with such a product.

Judge Solomon found in favour of the Defendant.

In his verbal Opinion he reviewed all of the evidence and expressed the view that whilst he was concerned that the carpet as delivered was underweight according to established US practice, he had been persuaded by the evidence that, on the balance of probabilities, the cause of the failure was the application of the silicone protector.

The Judge also said '.....one of the experts, Dr Britannica, for whatever reason, saw fit to assume the role of advocate rather than of an impartial and unbiased witness. And *this must be considered in evaluating his testimony and his credibility.*[7] For reasons known only to him, he voluntarily and without any response or urging of counsel saw fit to virtually charge [the manufacturer] with deceptive if not fraudulent practices. And I see nothing in the evidence or in this process that would warrant such an unfounded conclusion on his part.'[8]

---

[7] My italics.

[8] There is a lesson to be learned by all expert witnesses from these comments. As we have already noted, the duty of the expert witness is to serve the Court by explaining the technical issues and thus enable the Judge to reach a decision. It is not to accuse the other party of malpractice.

THE CASE OF THE DISASTROUS DELAMINATION

A 45 ounce pile weight tufted carpet of some 5500 square metres and manufactured in Japan was installed on four floors of the offices of a multinational corporation whose North American operations were managed from their offices in Vancouver BC.

Within three months of installation the customer complained that severe delamination was occurring with the face fabric separating from the secondary backing to such an extent that the installation presented a severe trip hazard in a number of places around the building.

The manufacturer submitted the carpet for testing by an independent laboratory in Japan, who found that the delamination strength was well within commercially acceptable tolerances.

Armed with these results, the importer rejected the claim on the basis that the normal performance of the carpet was satisfactory and that delamination was only occurring at seams which were beneath castor chairs. This aspect, he explained was not covered by warranty.

The customer was not happy with this explanation and arranged an independent inspection.

EXAMINATION	NOTES
An *in situ* examination, in the presence of the installer, confirmed that serious delamination was taking place beneath castor chairs. There were many examples on all floors where this was the case. However evidence of delamination in corridors could also be found. This was a reason for serious concern and tended to confirm the customer's view that the carpet was defective.	Castor chairs play havoc with tufted carpets and delamination is not uncommon. That is why many manufacturers, including the one in the present case, gave no warranty of performance in this respect. The customer is expected to protect the carpet with chair pads - typically polypropylene 'mats' that are placed over the carpet and under the castors.
Samples from five unused rolls of attic stock were taken for laboratory examination.	It is common practice in North America for additional carpet to be purchased when a large installation is carpeted. This material is known as attic stock.
Two series of tests were carried out. One was to determine the total mass and the other the pile mass above the substrate. In these tests the test results showed that the carpet met the details of the specification as demanded by the customer.	Total mass is the total product weight per square metre. Pile mass above the substrate is the pile weight above the backing usually obtained by shearing.
Tests were then undertaken to determine the delamination force. A value of only 5.3 Newtons was recorded for one of the samples and the maximum value recorded was 10.9 N. Such poor results clearly explained the delamination that was occurring on site although they clearly contradicted the results obtained by the Japanese laboratory.	The delamination force is the force required to separate the primary backing from the secondary backing. British Standard 7131 requires a minimum performance of 15N for a carpet intended for heavy domestic or general commercial use.
	Poor delamination strength also infers that there will be poor dimensional stability as the face fabric separates from its secondary backing and begins to stretch. A typical response to such extension is to call in an installer to restretch the carpet. Such a remedy is pointless since the face is inelastic and in theory will continue to grow in size until ultimately it falls apart.
	Poor delamination strength also leads to loss of tuft bind with consequent shedding of tufts.

[On the basis of the tests the customer believed that he had a genuine claim against

72

EXAMINATION

NOTES

the manufacturer. The value of the claim at that time (1990) was estimated at $800,000 given the disruption and associated costs involved. However, the corporate lawyer for the customer was concerned that the Court would look unfavourably upon them should they sue without giving the manufacturer an opportunity to put the matter right. Knowing this, the manufacturer had offered without prejudice *to undertake repairs at his own expense.]*

The inspector should remember that a Court might well expect the party who is in the right to give those liable an opportunity to put matters right without necessarily demanding replacement. Indeed the inspector can often offer to broker a deal that each party can accept.

With the results to hand a meeting was arranged to establish whether a repair could be carried out satisfactorily.

The meeting was held in the offices of the client's lawyer between the lawyer, the manufacturer's lawyer, an installer retained by the manufacturer, and the client's technical representative. At this meeting it was proposed that the delaminated areas of the carpet should be readhered to the secondary backing using a suitable adhesive to be agreed.

The installer suggested lifting the carpet, glueing the underlay to the floor, glueing the secondary backing to the underlay and glueing the primary backing to the secondary backing. A variation on the double stick technique which may be regarded as a triple glue down method!)

This option was rejected by the technical expert as being too unreliable on such a large scale. However, the legal representative of the client advised acceptance of a trial area of half of one floor so that the client could show the Court that he had been as accommodating as possible in trying to reach a mutually acceptable solution.

Given that the decision no longer rested with the technical expert a series of questions were posed nevertheless.

These sought to establish:

1. How the manufacturer intended to overcome any increase in dimensions that might occur because the primary backing had stretched.

2. Whether there was enough attic stock

EXAMINATION

to replace areas that were beyond repair? (at seams)

3.   How the manufacturer intended to deal with the fact that attic stock being used for the repair was itself faulty.

4.   Whether it was expected that further delamination would yet take place in areas that had not yet broken down.

5.   How the wear characteristics and appearance retention characteristics would be affected in the repaired areas.

6.   How much time should be allowed to elapse before the success of the trial could be judged.

In total, 23 questions were asked.

The answers were scarcely acceptable yet a date for the work to be undertaken was fixed accordingly.

In due course the trial was carried out and a third meeting of the various parties was initiated. The client was mostly dissatisfied because the carpet in the treated areas acquired a lumpy appearance not at all in keeping with the prestige image that it was meant to convey at the time of purchase.

On this basis, and following a third independent inspection, it seemed reasonable for the client to pursue the case for compensation through the legal system. However......

NOTES

By this stage it was becoming obvious that the client, despite their corporate strength was loathe to pursue the matter through the Courts. It subsequently transpired that the manufacturer was a 'tufter without machines' that is to say a company (of only six employees though part of a giant of the chemical industry) who sold carpet which they had made on commission by other manufacturers. It was clear to the client's corporate lawyer that if a legal action once started, the parent company would liquidate the carpet manufacturer and there would be no-one to sue. The issues were finally summarised in a letter from the client to their technical representative along the lines:

'The general terms of the settlement are a modest payment to us, repair of the carpet as necessary over the next 7 - 8 years and storage without charge of our attic stock until 1998. Given the diverse nature of the parties involved and the difficult financial situation in [our industry] at present, the settlement is a practical resolution to the matter.'

You can't win 'em all

THE CASE OF THE DIABOLICAL DRAUGHTMARKS

The case in question concerned an apartment in Mayfair throughout which an expensive 100% white wool carpet had been installed in every room. The walls were decorated with silk fabric wall coverings. The carpet and walls were turning black at such an alarming rate that the occupier was no longer able to live there. (The extent of the problem is shown in Plate IX). Legal proceedings had been commenced against the landlord and various engineers had undertaken major structural surveys which included and examination of air conditioning flues and ducts and had involved the lifting of floorboards.

EXAMINATION

Severe soiling was apparent throughout the entire apartment. This soiling affected the carpet, soft furnishings, wall coverings and fixtures and fittings.

With regard to the carpet the soiling was apparent in three ways:

1.   Extensive soiling around the edges of the carpet in the lounge and the bedroom.

2.   Extensive soiling beneath large pieces of furniture such as the bed and the settee.

3.   General overall soiling of all exposed areas of the carpet.

Additionally, it was observed that there was a portion of the carpet which was relatively unaffected by the general soiling. This was evident as a band approximately 50 mm wide running parallel to the direction of manufacture.

EDAX tests (Energy Dispersive X-Ray Analysis) showed that the contamination was soot.

Plate XI shows a piece of new unused carpet resting on the damaged, installed carpet.

NOTES

The primary issue however was to establish the source. The evidence of the unaffected band, which was found to coincide with tape joining the underlay, suggests at first sight that the air is passing from below the floor-boards, and the tape is masking the pile from exposure to the dirty air. However, it is fairly obvious after some thought that the air could be passing from above and escaping through the floor rather than originating below the floor. Indeed this is the important aspect of the case because the final conclusion would affect the outcome of the litigation in progress.

In normal circumstances the presence of draughtmarks, such as may cause the 'tele-graphing' of floorboards for example, is usually attributed to greasy air coming through the floor. The marks are then explained in terms of dirt trafficked in under foot adhering to the grease which has wicked to the tips of the tufts. This explains why the soil is only visible on the tips of the tufts.

However the same result would be observed if the dirt was present in the atmosphere and was forced down through the pile to pass top to bottom through the gaps in the floorboards.

EXAMINATION

Extensive examination indicated that there were areas where the soil, though worst at the surface, had penetrated the entire length of the tuft. The position of these areas in the room was noted.

The carpet was then uplifted and the underlay was examined in those places where the penetration of the tuft with dirt was total In several instances it was clear that a similar pattern of soiling could also be seen on the underlay.

NOTES

Since there was no way in which the underlay could have been soiled by foot traffic, it is fairly safe to assume that the soil was passing from top to bottom. In other words dirty air in the room was being drawn through gaps in the floor because air pressure in the room volume was greater than that in the floor void no doubt because of the mechanics of the air conditioning system. Such severe contamination of the walls and soft furnishings tends to bear out this view.

This begs the question as to why the air in the room was so dirty in the first place.

There are two possible explanations. One is that the general atmosphere in the city centre is laden with oily substances that were inefficiently filtered out by the air conditioning, (which drew approximately 10% of its intake form outside). The other is that the air conditioning system was itself creating the sooty deposits that were being circulated round the room. The answer to these questions were left to the plant engineers.

The case is important however because it demonstrates that what at first appears to be an ordinary instance of draughtmarking is not always so and the conventional wisdom that draughtmarking originates beneath the floorboards and gaps in the skirting, should not be taken for granted.

US Glossary.
Underlay = Padding or Cushion
Draughtmarking = Filtration Soiling
Skirting = Baseboard

THE CASE OF THE FIBRILLATING FIBRE

A coral coloured 100% wool carpet acquired a white flecked appearance in the traffic lanes. This flecking was completely removed by cleaning however. (Plate XII).

In subsequent use, the flecks reappeared, though once more they were easily removed by cleaning. And so the cycle continued.

FLOOR INSPECTION SERVICES LTD
Chorlton cum Hardy

25 December 199x

Anytime Cleaners Ltd
Somewhere
Over the Rainbow

Dear Sirs,

Examination of coral carpet

We have now completed our examination of the off-cut from your client's carpet which changes shade upon trafficking. We understand however that the nature of this shade change is not consistent with that which normally occurs upon flattening but is manifest by the development of white flecks across all traffic lanes. We further understand that cleaning restores the carpet to an almost new appearance but that the flecks reappear as the carpet is again trafficked.

We ourselves have cleaned a specimen showing the fault and can confirm that we have observed the same improvement in our laboratory tests. We waited three weeks for the flecks to reappear but, without any trafficking, they did not. Subsequent light abrasion in a Hexapod Tumbler Tester caused the cleaned specimen to change in the way you describe.

Microscopical examination of fibres taken from the pile yarn showed that many were ruptured and split.

It is our opinion that the wool fibre has been damaged during wet processing in yarn form probably with alkali or bleach.[1] [2] As the carpet is trafficked the degraded wool fibrillates, causing a change in the light reflectance characteristics. This produces an apparent lightening in shade. Subsequent cleaning physically removes the broken fibre ends and the appearance is therefore restored until it is trafficked again and further damage occurs.

Clearly, the wear characteristics of this carpet are unacceptable and it should be replaced.

Yours faithfully,

E Morse (Inspector)

---

[1] Confirmatory solubility tests subsequently confirmed that this was the case.
[2] Fearing that the client or manufacturer may blame him, the cleaner wrote back to ask for confirmation that this effect could not be caused by cleaning under alkaline conditions. He knew he had never cleaned the carpet under alkaline conditions but thought he might be accused of doing so. We had no difficulty in giving this confirmation. - This degree of damage could only have arisen during wet processing in yarn form.

PLATES

Typical appearance of 'Sporadic Spot'

SPORADIC SPOTS

Plate I

Photomicrograph of soil adhering to fibres (1)

SPORADIC SPOTS

Plate II

Photomicrograph of soil adhering to fibres (2)

SPORADIC SPOTS

Plate III

Colour difference between nylon and polypropylene component of tile

BICOMPONENT BLUNDER

Plate IV

Colour fastness test results

BURGUNDY BLEEDER

Plate V

Total breakdown of backing yarns

MANIC MECHANIC

Plate VI

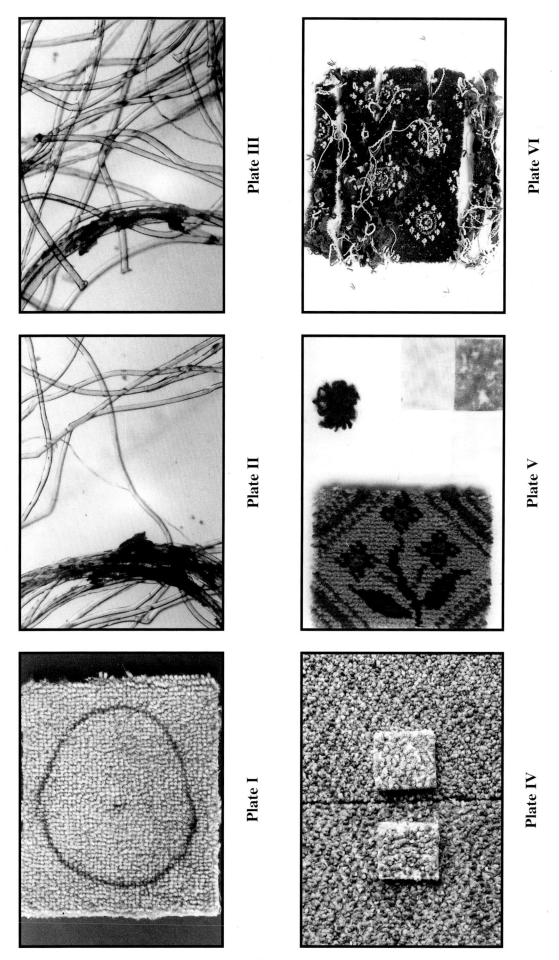

Plate III

Plate VI

Plate II

Plate V

Plate I

Plate IV

83

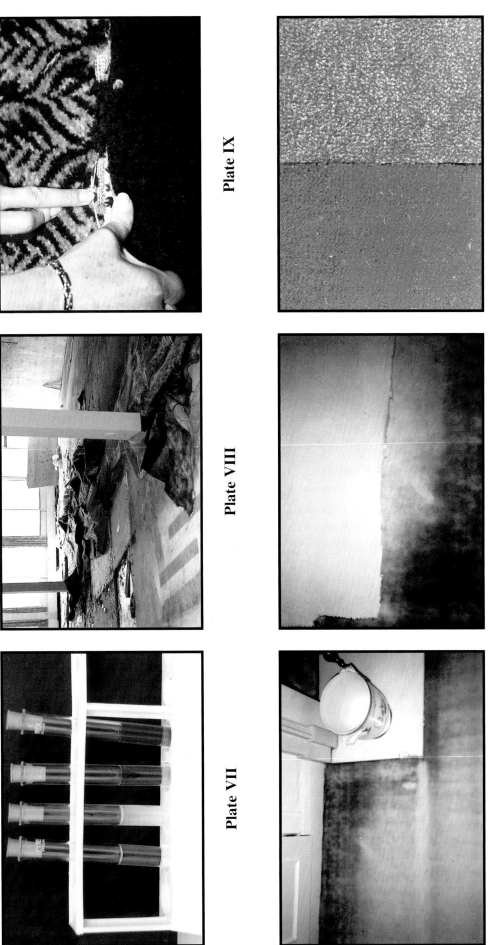

Plate IX

Plate VIII

Plate VII

Plate XII

Plate XI

Plate X

84

Tests for pH and sulphate on normal and faulty carpet

MANIC MECHANIC

Plate VII

Hurricane Bob comes to town

LITIGIOUS LAWYER

Plate VIII

Example of poor seaming technique

LITIGIOUS LAWYER

Plate IX

Draughtmarks in front of hearth

DIABOLICAL DRAUGHTMARKS

Plate X

New carpet resting on top of draughtmarked carpet

DIABOLICAL DRAUGHTMARKS

Plate XI

Change is shade upon cleaning

FIBRILLATING FIBRE

Plate XII